Resurrection & Me

SAINT **SHENOUDA**PRESS

Resurrection & Me

Fr Bishoy Kamel

Translated By
Yvonne Tadros

ST SHENOUDA PRESS
SYDNEY, AUSTRALIA
2019

Resurrection & Me

Fr Bishoy Kamel

ST SHENOUDA PRESS
8419 Putty Rd,
Putty, NSW, 2330
Sydney, Australia

www.stshenoudapress.com

ISBN 13: 978-0-6482814-9-8

Translated by:
Yvonne Tadros

Contents

Contents

Translator's Note:

These sermons were written in colloquial Egyptian Arabic. I tried my best to translate them for the English reader according to English sentence structure, with adherence to meaning in the Arabic version and at the same time reflecting the spirituality therein, as this booklet is part of a series of sermons by the Rev. Hegumenos Bishoy Kamel. Proper nouns are transliterated. There may also be spelling variations.

Biblical Quote References are from NIV or NKJV depending on which is closest to the Arabic Version.

Section One

Resurrection Sermons

Introduction

HOW DO WE LIVE THE RESURRECTION?

The coming of Christ our Lord to the world, His Crucifixion and His Resurrection—these events were always intended to serve a greater purpose than simply resurrecting us from our graves at the end of the world. Had a physical resurrection been our Lord's sole intention, His spoken word would have sufficed to rise all the bodies on Earth—whether good or evil—from their graves.

Of Christ's resurrection, John 5:28-29 says, "Do not marvel at this; for the hour is coming in which all who are in the graves will hear His voice and come forth—those who have done good, to the resurrection of life, and those who have done evil, to the resurrection of condemnation".

Christ the Lord described Himself as "The Resurrection". He came to give the power of His Resurrection to mankind, raising us with Him in this existing world. He raised the dead inner soul of the sinner woman into a strong woman who stood triumphant over lust and weakness. This is an example of the First Resurrection.

Peter, too, was resurrected with Him after faltering cowardly before a maidservant. Despite Peter's claims to bravery, he vehemently denied Christ. However, this was the same Peter who rejoiced in being counted worthy to suffer shame for his name: "So they departed from the presence of the council, rejoicing that they were counted worthy to suffer shame for His name" (Acts 5:41). This was another example of the First Resurrection, whereby the Lord Jesus raised Peter with Him.

Similarly, the disciples were resurrected with Him. They were filled with fear and doubt when Jesus arrived among them, moving through closed doors to enter the room in which they were hiding, and yet, when Christ said, "Peace be with you", the disciples were filled with joy and courage: another example of the First Resurrection.

Thus, the Christian Resurrection is a Divine act within the soul, whereby the Holy Spirit transfers our souls into joyous and triumphant existence. If the Spirit of Him who raised Jesus from the dead dwells in you, He who raised Christ from the dead will also give life to your mortal body. This experience is the Christian Resurrection. It is an eternal experience, beginning with Baptism, followed by burial with Christ and Resurrection with Him. In the book of Romans, Resurrection is described clearly: "Therefore, we were buried with Him through baptism into death, that just as Christ was raised from the dead by the glory of the Father, even so we also should walk in newness of life" (Romans 6:4).

Through constant daily repentance, we attain resurrection: "...

knowing that He who raised up the Lord Jesus will also raise us up with Jesus, and will present us with you... Therefore we do not lose heart. Even though our outward man is perishing, yet the inward man is being renewed day by day". (2 Corinthians 4:14-16)

We gain a resurrected life in the sacrament of the Eucharist, which is the Resurrection. Further, we are raised through acts of love because those who love are moved from death to life: "We know that we have passed from death to life, because we love each other. Anyone who does not love remains in death" (1 John 3:14).

We also gain hope through resurrection: "Yes, we had the sentence of death in ourselves, that we should not trust in ourselves but in God who raises the dead, who delivered us from so great a death, and does deliver us; in whom we trust that He will still deliver us" (2 Corinthians 1:9-10).

We gain the power of triumph over lust through resurrection: "And those who are Christ's have crucified the flesh with its passions and desires. If we live in the Spirit, let us also walk in the Spirit" (Galatians 5:24).

We gain bravery, conquer fear, and experience liberty through resurrection: "The Spirit of the Lord is upon Me, because He has anointed Me to preach the gospel to the poor; He has sent Me to heal the broken-hearted, to proclaim liberty to the captive and recovery of sight to the blind, to set at liberty those who are oppressed" (Luke 4:18). As children of the light, we can walk in the light through resurrection: "But he who does the truth comes to the light, that his deeds may be clearly seen, that they have been done in God" (John 3:21).

Finally, we are empowered to evangelise and minister through resurrection: "Go therefore and make disciples of all the nations, baptizing them in the name of the Father and of the Son and of the Holy Spirit" (Mt 28:19).

Resurrection is the experience of the Christian's whole life. It is not a theatrical play performed only on the Feast of the Resurrection—it is a continuous, daily act.

It is untrue that, as some claim, the period of Pentecost is one of laxity, gluttony, and luke-warmness. In fact, those who experience the First Resurrection feel that the period of Pentecost is more than the fifty days after the Resurrection: rather, it is our whole life until our souls cross over to heaven.

Blessed is he who has part in the First Resurrection, over such the second death has no power but they shall be priests of God and of Christ and shall reign with Him a thousand years. Amen.

Hegumen Bishoy Kamel

The Procession and the Resurrection Icon

During the liturgy of the Resurrection Feast and the liturgies of the Holy fifty days, the Priests and Deacons walk around the church three times in their royal garments, offering incense before the icon of the Resurrection. Throughout this time, the entire congregation sings joyously and triumphantly: "Christ is risen from the dead. With His death He crushed death. He gave those who were dead eternal life."

This is a procession of three living icons participating with Christ's Resurrection. The First Icon is the one before which the Priest offers incense. This icon is anointed with holy oil radiating the live-giving spirit of the Resurrection and filling the whole church with power and great glory.

The Second Icon is traditional, in that the baptism of the catechumens (their burial followed by their resurrection in baptism) took place on the night of the Feast of the Resurrection. The Church then paraded the catechumens in the icon's procession, thus becoming the Second Icon on the night of the Feast of the Resurrection, having been raised with Christ from the dead—and how magnificent is the Second Icon. The Church lives in the Resurrection.

The Third Icon is the most magnificent of all the icons. It is the Church who lives the power of the Resurrection with Christ through a life of repentance and death to the world. At this point in the liturgy, each soul in the church sings loudly: "Christ rose us with Him. He broke the thorn of death and gave us life".

How beautiful is the Church whose whole congregation leads a life of repentance with the Resurrected Christ? Such a congregation is a living icon of the Resurrected Christ. This is the living procession of the Resurrection, during which time we sing the triumphing hymn of salvation. This is also the hymn of our death to the world:

"Christ is risen and raised us up with Him.
He crushed death by His own death.
He blessed us with eternal life,
We who were dead in the tombs of sin."

As Christians, during the Resurrection Prayers, let us make our lives a true icon of the Resurrected Christ. Indeed, let us be holy and joyous all the days of our life.

The First Resurrection and the Biblical Texts

We realise that Christ's Resurrection was for the purpose of renewing our fallen and sinful souls. With that in mind, here are some biblical instances that describe the life bestowed through the First Resurrection.

1. The Raising of Lazarus

The Lord Jesus told Martha that her brother would rise. Martha said to Him, "I know that he will rise again in the resurrection at the last day." Jesus said to her, "I am the resurrection and the life. He who believes in Me, though he may die, he shall live. And whoever lives and believes in Me shall never die. Do you believe this?" (John 11:24-26).

In His discussion with Martha, we see our Lord Jesus drawing a distinction between the two resurrections. The First Resurrection pertains to those who are physically alive on earth "... whoever lives and believes in Me shall never die..." The Second Resurrection pertains to those who have passed away and are buried: "He who believes in Me, though he may die, he shall live." Our Lord Jesus emphasises that those who believe in Him in this world will experience the power of the Resurrection in their lives.

2. The First and Second Resurrections

The First Resurrection occurs during our lifetime: "Most assuredly, I say to you, the hour is coming, and now is, when the dead will hear the voice of the Son of God; and those who hear will live" (John 5:25). Thus, having a resurrected life takes place through the person of Christ when we believe in Him and listen to His word.

The Second Resurrection is the Christian's resurrection from the grave: "... for the hour is coming in which all who are in the graves will hear His voice and come forth—those who have done good, to the resurrection of life, and those who have done evil, to the resurrection of condemnation" (John

5:28). The Lord Jesus Christ calls us now to hear the voice of His Gospel to the resurrection of life. Whoever does not hear His voice will not taste life.

3. Those who do not know Christ are dead

Saint John the Beloved stresses that all those who do not know Christ are dead spiritually. Further, those who are dead cannot be alive, except through their belief in Christ and their rejection of the Beast and his image.

And I saw thrones, and they sat on them, and judgment was committed to them. Then I saw the souls of those who had been beheaded for their witness to Jesus and for the word of God, who had not worshipped the beast or his image, and had not received his mark on their foreheads or on their hands. And they lived and reigned with Christ for [a]a thousand years. 5 But the rest of the dead did not live again until the thousand years were finished. This is the First Resurrection. 6 Blessed and holy is he who has part in the first resurrection. Over such the second death has no power, but they shall be priests of God and of Christ and shall reign with Him a thousand years. (Revelations 20:4-6)

This verse is a divine call to mankind to be dead to this world. We are called to live with Christ. In the First Resurrection, we rise with Christ, who died for our sins and rose to sanctify us and reign with Him for a thousand years.

4. The power of the Resurrection over death

The power of the Resurrection was manifested to such an extent that the disciples thought that John the Beloved would never see death. A person who is attached to Christ is full of His love and abides by the teachings of the Gospel. For these reasons, a person who is attached to Christ radiates the light, power and joy of the Resurrection.

For this reason, Peter asked our Lord Jesus about John. "Peter, seeing him, said to Jesus, 'But Lord, what about this man?' Jesus said to him, 'If I will that he remain till I come, what is that to you? You follow Me.' Then this saying went out among the brethren that this disciple would not die. Yet Jesus did not say to him that he would not die, but, 'If I will that he remain till I come, what is that to you?'" (John 21:21-23).

To Whom Does the Lord Reveal His Resurrection?

The crucifixion took place in broad daylight and full view of the public: anyone could walk to Golgotha to witness it. In contrast, only a few disciples and close members were fortunate to witness the Resurrection and the Ascension. Why was this the case? Witnessing the Resurrected Lord was God's privilege alone.

The Cross has a specific spot outside Jerusalem which is accessible to anyone. In contrast, the Resurrection has no location, since the Lord selects where and when to appear. The Cross also has a specific spot accessible to whoever wishes to partake in communion with Christ's love and sufferings. They will find Him with arms wide open saying, "Come unto me..."—and "Forgive them". They will see blood and water oozing from His open side, giving us life, healing and washing us from our sins.

The Manger has a specific spot accessible to anyone who

wishes to visit it to experience humility. The Transfiguration Mount also has a specific spot accessible to whoever wishes to ascend it prayerfully. Christians can visit these places at any time they choose. In contrast, the Resurrection has no specific physical location, nor does it have any specific time because it is the apparition of God in our lives according to His generous grace.

The Lord may appear within our homes when we least expect Him, even if the doors are shut. He may appear while we are walking down a street suffering the pain of loneliness and abandonment. He may also appear while we suffer the pain of His absence, like the disciples in Emmaus, or during the frustrating weariness of a fruitless day when we fail to catch any fish.

The fact is that we have no say as to where and when the Lord appears. However, this does not mean that His presence is an exclusive privilege granted to a fortunate few. On the contrary, His presence is easily accessible because it is the Lord Himself who makes the effort of coming to us in the following situations:

The Lord appears to souls who, through Baptism, are baptised into Him: "Or do you not know that as many of us as were baptized into Christ Jesus were baptized into His death? Therefore, we were buried with Him through baptism into death, that just as Christ was raised from the dead by the glory of the Father, even so we also should walk in newness of life. For if we have been united together in the likeness of His death, certainly we also shall be in the likeness of His resurrection. (Romans 6:3-5)

Thus, the person who believes wholeheartedly that one is buried completely with Christ through Baptism also believes that the old being is buried and a new being arises; the person who embraces this belief dies to the sin in which we were born. The person who embraces Baptism fervently will witness the Resurrected Christ constantly throughout their life and will grow in grace through the power of His Resurrection. This is the belief in which we live throughout our temporary life on Earth.

The Lord appears to resurrect repentant souls. Whoever leads a life of repentance, carrying their cross while overcoming all the obstacles that impede their walk alongside Christ, is worthy of witnessing the dawn of the resurrection of Lord Jesus. Each soul who battles against sin and loves Christ is worthy of witnessing His glory and being in His embrace, just like the Prodigal Son.

The loving Lord sees that battling souls remain worthy of His reassuring extended hand despite their weaknesses and failures. They are worthy of being resurrected and receiving Christ's revelation. These souls—who have crucified their desires—are worthy of saying "I have been crucified with Christ; it is no longer I who live, but Christ lives in me" (Galatians 2:20).

The Lord appears to those who walk with Him all the way up to Golgotha. Whoever walks with Christ all the way up to Golgotha (like Stephen, who suffered the hatred of the world and the pains of stoning) is worthy of seeing the sky opened and the Son of Man seated on the right hand of the Father.

For this reason, martyrs remain joyful and jubilant regardless of the sufferings they endure. So do God's children, who endure ordeals thankfully and happily in partnership with the Lord's sufferings. Those who persevere will witness the Lord's apparition in glory at the end of their walk.

The Lord appears to those who seek Him with fervent love. Recall the women who walked to the tomb eagerly carrying their perfume: the Lord Himself appeared to them, saying "Rejoice!" Thus, the women came and held Him by the feet and worshipped Him. Likewise, the souls whose worship of the Lord is combined with fragrant feelings and deep love of Christ will inevitably see the Lord and rejoice when they hear the voice saying, "He is risen".

The Lord appears to those who fish the whole night in vain. He appears to those who toil hard all night, trying strenuously to fish without losing hope, trusting that the Lord will appear in the end. Those who serve for years with perseverance and honesty are bound to see the fruits at the end of their long night. The Lord Himself will provide them with fish and honey from the very fruit of their blessed toil.

The Resurrection is a path through which we walk daily. We experience it each time we carry our cross joyfully and without complaint.

The Resurrection and the Church Sacraments

The Sacrament of Baptism

Baptism is the pigment with which we are dyed. Baptism replaces the pigment of death: through it, we acquire the life of resurrection. Baptism is the sacred engraving of death to sin and worldly evil. Baptism is what the Church engraves on us, leading the power of Christ's life and Resurrection to move within us. "For if we have been united together in the likeness of His death, certainly we also shall be in the likeness of His resurrection" (Rom. 6:5).

Baptism is the lethal weapon against sin. The great sinners (like Augustine and Moses the Black) overcame their sin, emerging as sons of Resurrection and Life. The Bible teaches us this in the following examples: "And have put on the new man who is renewed in knowledge according to the image of Him who created him" (Colossian 3:10) and, "Therefore, we were buried with Him through baptism into death, that just as Christ was raised from the dead by the glory of the Father, even so we also should walk in newness of life" (Romans 6:3-4).

It is impossible for those resurrected in Christ to be overcome by death. Thus, the Apostle says: "... knowing that Christ, having been raised from the dead, dies no more ... Likewise, you also, reckon yourselves to be dead indeed to sin, but alive to God in Christ Jesus our Lord. Therefore, do not let sin reign in your mortal body, that you should obey it in its lusts. And do not present your members as instruments of unrighteousness to sin, but present yourselves to God as being alive from the dead, and your members as instruments of righteousness to God. For sin shall not have dominion over you, for you are not under law but under grace" (Romans 6:9-14).

This point is also emphasised in Romans 6:4: "Therefore we were buried with Him through baptism into death, that just as Christ was raised from the dead by the glory of the Father, even so we also should walk in newness of life", and again in Colossians 2:12: "... buried with Him in baptism, in which you also were raised with Him through faith in the working of God, who raised Him from the dead".

The procession of the baptised
The Church strongly regards the Baptism as entailing the participation of each of us in death and resurrection with Christ. Thus, we parade the baptised within the Church as we would a living icon of the Resurrection, all the while singing Áxios—"worthy". On the eve of the Feast of the Resurrection, it is tradition for the baptised to be paraded around the church three times in a procession. During this Resurrection

procession, the Baptised (the catechumens) sing Christos Anesti —"Christ is risen".

The location of the font in the Church

The Church rite describes that the baptismal font should be located at the entry of the Church in order to be seen by Christians as they enter—but is it possible to adopt the baptismal font location as a spiritual practice to reflect on the Resurrection? The answer is yes: each time we enter the Church, we can pause for a moment before the font, professing, "Here we were buried and each day we walk through life dying to sin". In this moment, the dawn of the first Resurrection shines in our new resurrected life, making us God's heavenly children.

Next time you enter the church, try this practice, whereby the ritual and the first Resurrection become a life. When you stand before the font, remember that you have:

- denounced Satan and all his impure practices

- removed your old self and put on a new one, which is according to the image of your Creator

- become one with Christ in likeness with His death and Resurrection

- died, been buried and Resurrected with Christ

- become a tool of goodness before God through your resurrection

- recognised that Resurrection amounts to being serious in daily life

- been born from above as God's child. Thus, you draw your own path in life towards a happy eternity.

The Sacrament of Chrismation is the Spirit of the Resurrection

When pausing before the font, reflect that you were anointed with the chrism like the historical Kings. You were anointed not only with sacred oil, but with a chrism made of perfumes and embalms placed on the body of the Lord, the life-giver who was resurrected from the dead. You have now become an altar through this sacred ointment, which is the spirit of the Resurrection. Hence, you are consecrated just like a physical altar. Your whole body is consecrated, so treat your body with the respect and dignity it is due.

Chrismation is the spirit of the Resurrection:
"But if the Spirit of Him who raised Jesus from the dead dwells in you, He who raised Christ from the dead will also give life to your mortal bodies through His Spirit who dwells in you" (Romans 8:11). Chrismation teaches us all: "But the anointing which you have received from Him abides in you, and you do not need that anyone teach you; but as the same anointing teaches you concerning all things, and is true, and is not a lie, and just as it has taught you, you will abide in Him" (1 John 2:27).

Chrismation sets our minds on things above: "Set your mind on things above, not on things on the earth" (Colossians 3:2). It is this Spirit who takes what is of Christ and gives us the fruit of the Spirit.

My Lord Jesus:
I thank You for making me Your Altar. The filth of my body is worse than the filth of the manger in Bethlehem. Have mercy

on me. Purify my altar from all impurity; expel the money-changers so that the altar may become solely yours.

O comforting Spirit of the Resurrection, may you always watch over my constant repentance. O' Spirit of Guidance, may You open my mind to understand what is written and perceive the depth of your mysteries. O' Spirit of Love, may You pour Your divine love in my heart.

"Now hope does not disappoint, because the love of God has been poured out in our hearts by the Holy Spirit who was given to us" (Romans 5:5).

O' Holy Spirit, the Promise of the Father, reveal to me my new place on the right hand of the Father. O' Holy Spirit, bear witness within me to enable me to say "Abba, Father". How can I feel your paternity, O' Father, except through Your Spirit within me?

O' Holy Spirit, may You burst all your good life-giving fruits through the shut doors within my soul. O' Holy Spirit, the treasure of goodness, enrich my life with Your presence which is concealed within me. Enrich my life with prayer, life, joy, meekness, and constant penitence.

"... As poor, yet making many rich; as having nothing, and yet possessing all things" (2 Corinthians 6:10).

The Sacrament of Repentance

The sacrament of repentance is linked to the resurrection, since sin amounts to falling and repentance amounts to rising. In fact, repentance is indispensable to each sacrament: the first resurrection (repentance) is foundational to each sacrament. This sacrament is the gateway to Christianity. Repentance precedes each sacrament, and so repentance also precedes Baptism. In turn, Baptism becomes a continual act.

First, recall the Acts of the Apostles, which emphasised the necessity of repentance before Baptism and the receiving of Christ: "Then Peter said to them, 'Repent, and let every one of you be baptized in the name of Jesus Christ for the remission of sins; and you shall receive the gift of the Holy Spirit'" (Acts 2:38).

Repentance is what distinguishes Christianity from any other belief system. For Christians, repentance precedes Baptism and raises a person to new life. Without this sacrament, how can one arise in the First Resurrection while remaining in a fallen state?

Precisely for this reason, the early Church did not rush to receive non-believers into the Christian faith. Instead, non-believers were required to persevere in a genuinely repentant life—an end that could take years to achieve. In contrast, institutions and leaders of other belief systems might have accepted non-believers more readily.

For Christians who receive the sacrament of the First Resurrection during childhood, this First Resurrection ought to continue throughout their life, in the form of a second baptism practised with daily tears.

The Prodigal Son received the grace of adoption through baptism. Subsequently, he left for a distant country, where he fell into sin and took care of pigs. Thankfully, he washed himself with repentant tears and returned to his Father's embrace to enjoy his previous life.

The practice of continuity of repentance led the Apostle Saint Paul to say: "For Your sake we are killed all day long; we are accounted as sheep for the slaughter" (Romans 8:36), and "always carrying about in the body the dying of the Lord Jesus, that the life of Jesus also may be manifested in our body" (2 Corinthians 4:10). Saint Paul also added: "I affirm, by the boasting in you which I have in Christ Jesus our Lord, I die daily" (1 Corinthians 15:31).

Repentance amounts to experiencing, each day and in each moment, our own First Resurrection with Christ. Whoever neglects repentance loses the power of the Resurrection because they lead a fallen and lukewarm life.

In order to repent meaningfully and continually, a Christian should consider the following questions:

- Is my Resurrection daily with Christ?
- Is my Baptism daily, which washes my garments?
- Is the way whereby the Resurrection works (that is, via the Holy Spirit) within me every moment

And, without repentance:

- Am I able to live the Resurrection?
- Are there any other means of cherishing Christ and His Father's embrace?
- Am I able to receive the Sacrament of the Eucharist and Resurrection?
- Am I able to live as a resurrected Christian?
- Am I able to taste the Crucifixion and the Resurrection?

Christians should also remember that it is through repentance that...

- One reaps the fruit of the Holy Spirit.

- The Father rejoices, runs, and embraces His son.

- The Son rejoices. He carries the lamb on His shoulders despite His weariness.

- The Holy Spirit rejoices upon finding the lost coin.

- The angels in heaven rejoice.

- The saints rejoice.

What then is the significance of the Resurrection for the contrite soul?

1. Confidence in Repentance
The Disciples lived in fear at one stage. After the Resurrection, they not only overcame their fear—their entire lives were transferred into courage and joy. Recall that Paul and Silas were overjoyed when they were in prison "... Paul and Silas were praying and singing hymns to God, and the prisoners were listening to them" (Acts 16:25).

After the Resurrection, the Disciples who had lost their faith after the crucifixion believed again. Thomas became a Christian evangelist, his doubts transforming into a firm belief, while Peter became a shepherd of Christ's flock:

"Let him who stole steal no longer, but rather let him labour, working with his hands what is good, that he may have something to give him who has need. Let no corrupt word proceed out of your mouth, but what is good for necessary edification, that it may impart grace to the hearers. And do not grieve the Holy Spirit of God, by whom you were sealed for the day of redemption. Let all bitterness, wrath, anger, clamour, and evil speaking be put away from you, with all malice. And be kind to one another, tender-hearted, forgiving one another, even as God in Christ forgave you" (Ephesians 4:28-32).

Clearly, repentance is a positive act—one that extends beyond merely refraining from evil, but encompasses a yearning to do well.

2. Repentance is Resurrection through the Cross
It is not possible to experience the power of the Resurrection unless one experiences carrying his cross and the suffering involved in doing so: "I have been crucified with Christ; it is no longer I who live, but Christ lives in me" (Galatians 2:20).

The characteristics that accompany carrying the cross all lead to the joys of the Resurrection. The light of the cross shines in the lives of all those who experience fasting, prayer, and sacrifice for Christ's sake. This is because the cross is the only way to Resurrection.

When Thomas touched the wounds of Christ and later reflected on the Lord's sufferings, it was as if the whole light of the Resurrection had shone in his life. Following His Resurrection, God appeared only to those who accompanied Him during His suffering—even for a short time only: "... if indeed we suffer with Him, that we may also be glorified together" (Romans 8:17).

3. Joy and Peace: Symbols of the Resurrection

"Peace I leave with you, My peace I give to you; not as the world gives do I give to you. Let not your heart be troubled, neither let it be afraid". The Resurrection bestows the peace of Christ to the repentant. The repentant person receives joy that no one can diminish—his sadness is turned into joy.

Repentance is an extension of Baptism—it is a resurrection and a birth: "A woman, when she is in labour, has sorrow because her hour has come; but as soon as she has given birth to the child, she no longer remembers the anguish, for joy that a human being has been born into the world" (John 16:21). This is the fruit of the repentant, a new birth that generates joy and peace.

4. Repentance and Resurrection: Return to the Father's Embrace

"I will arise and go to my father, and will say to him, "Father, I have sinned against heaven and before you" (Luke 15:18). Repentance amounts to rising—rising like the body of Christ, who rose, ascended after forty days and sat on the right hand of the Father. In a Christian's life, the ultimate aim of rising is being in the Father's embrace.

When we bear in mind that Baptism is the First Resurrection, and Baptism is our adoption to the grace of the Father, we recognise that the glory of repentance and resurrection is incomplete until we join the Father's embrace. We are called through the Holy Spirit to repent by saying "Abba" (Father). Through repentance, we rise joyously in the bosom of the Father, attaining peace and purity. Thus, the repentant Christian becomes led by the Spirit of the Father: "For as

many as are led by the Spirit of God, these are sons of God"
(Romans 8:14).

The Icon of the Penitent
When the fallen soul rises, it radiates a great power—a power
that stems from the Lord's Resurrection. Consider these
examples:

- Moses the Black was a murderer and adulterer and
  changed completely after his repentance. Think of his
  mighty power after his conversion.

- Strong Baeisa, who repented after leading a life of
  prostitution. Her icon was like a pillar of fire in the sky.

- The icon of Maria the Egyptian, a prostitute who ended
  up being an anchorite in the Jordanian wilderness.

- The portrait of Tais, who led hundreds of young men
  to fall into sin before becoming a recluse worshiper,
  spending many nights in prayer, fasting, and tears.

- The icon of the sinful woman repentant at the feet of
  Jesus, kissing and washing His feet with her tears. She
  was mightier than all the members of Herod's palace
  and his royal family.

These icons of Repentance are mighty and magnificent—
the most profound icons of the Christian faith. Their stories
resonate with so many Christians, like the most beautiful
tunes coming from the depth of the tomb: "Christ is risen!
Truly He is risen! He is risen from among the dead. Through
His death, He crushed Death, giving eternal life to those in
graves!"

The Lord's Body is Communion with Resurrection

There is a strong link between the Resurrection and receiving the Body and Blood of the Lord. This link is so strong that we can say: "When we partake of Christ's body, we partake of His Resurrection". The Church, in turn, during the Holy fifty days, dedicates her teachings to the Lord's Body and His Blood. The intention being conveyed is that Resurrection amounts to receiving the Lord's Body and Blood, as said in the liturgy: "Each time you eat this bread... You profess the resurrection of The Lord".

In the following simple reflections upon the Eucharist, readers can experience Christ Resurrected from among the dead.

1. The Start of the Week

Traditionally, the early Church offered the sacrament of the Eucharist on the first day of the week: Sunday. Why was Sunday chosen as the first day of the week? Because Sunday is the day of Christ's resurrection. Taking the Lord's body is life-giving; it is the practical extension of the Resurrection in our life: "Now on the first day of the week, when the disciples came together to break bread ..." or, "Now the first day of the week Mary Magdalene went to the tomb early, while it was still dark, and saw that the stone had been taken away from the tomb" (John 20:1-18).

2. The Psalm of the Resurrection

"This is the day the Lord has made; we will rejoice and be glad in it" (Ps 118:24 NKJV). This is the Psalm said during the liturgy of the Feast of the Resurrection, which is also said every Sunday and throughout the Holy fifty days. Again, this

Psalm confirms the connection between the Eucharist and Sunday. Thus, the disciples assembled on Sunday in order to break bread. The day of the Resurrection "... is the day the Lord has made". It is the day of the Eucharist—the day of our resurrection, on which we rejoice in partaking of Christ's body.

3. Resurrection in the Eucharist

The Lord revealing His Resurrection in the Eucharist was evidenced clearly. At the moment of the breaking of bread, the eyes of the disciples were opened, and they became aware of His Resurrection. This is a wonderful connection: to see the Resurrected Lord from among the dead when we receive His Body and Blood.

"Then they drew near to the village where they were going, and He indicated that He would have gone farther. But they constrained Him, saying, 'Abide with us, for it is toward evening, and the day is far spent'. And He went in to stay with them. Now it came to pass, as He sat at the table with them, that He took bread, blessed and broke it, and gave it to them. Then their eyes were opened and they knew Him; and He vanished from their sight. And they said to one another, 'Did not our heart burn within us while He talked with us on the road, and while He opened the Scriptures to us?' So they rose up that very hour and returned to Jerusalem, and found the eleven and those who were with them gathered together, saying, 'The Lord is risen indeed, and has appeared to Simon!' And they told about the things that had happened on the road, and how He was known to them in the breaking of bread" (Luke 24:28-35).

Thus for Christians, the breaking of bread became an eye-opener to the Resurrection and the vision of Christ rising from the dead.

4. The Lord's Body is life and the Resurrection is life

Each time our Lord mentioned the Eucharist, He spoke about eternal life and His forgiveness of our sins:

- The Eucharist is given for the forgiveness of sins, and eternal life is given to those partake of Him. Those who detach from the Eucharist are deprived of Resurrection and eternal life as sin equals death; "unless you eat the flesh of the Son of Man and drink His blood, you have no life in you" (John 6:53).

- The Eucharist is also the transfusion of Christ's imperishable blood into our bodies.

The Young Man Named Eutychus

In the story of Eutychus we see two important aspects: death ("he was sinking into a deep sleep, he fell down from the third story and was taken up dead") and Resurrection and Christ's body being distributed by Paul ("Now when he had come up, had broken bread and ate they brought the young man in alive").

The resurrection of Eutychus from death to life is not merely a miracle of raising someone from the dead. It is a practical example that Christ's body is Resurrection, which overcomes death. For this reason, this incident is read on the second Sunday of the Holy fifty days, when the theme of the sermon is the Eucharist.

The Church determined that the second Sunday of the Holy fifty days was suited to a reading of the part of the Gospel regarding receiving the bread of life. In the Book of John (6:48-51), Jesus says, "I am the bread of life. Your fathers ate the manna in the wilderness, and are dead. This is the bread which comes down from heaven that one may eat of it and not die. I am the living bread which came down from heaven. If anyone eats of this bread, he will live forever; and the bread that I shall give is My flesh, which I shall give for the life of the world".

Abide in Me

It was mentioned earlier in this text that sin amounts to detachment from God, while Resurrection amounts to abiding in God. Hence, communion is the route to abiding in Him. Once the branch is detached from the vine, it withers and dies—as our Lord confirmed:

"Abide in Me, and I in you. As the branch cannot bear fruit of itself, unless it abides in the vine, neither can you, unless you abide in Me. I am the vine, you are the branches. He who abides in Me, and I in him, bears much fruit; for without Me you can do nothing" (Jn. 15:4-5—NKJV).

"Whoever eats My flesh and drinks My blood has eternal life, and I will raise him up at the last day. For My flesh is food indeed, and My blood is drink indeed. He who eats My flesh and drinks My blood abides in Me, and I in him" (Jn. 6:54-56 NKJV)

An ideal example of abiding in Christ is ensuring that a soul bears the fruits of the Holy Spirit. Consider the following

parable from the Book of John (titled: "The Life of Prayer"):
"When a farmer realises that a tree is weak and bears poor
fruit, he cuts a shoot from a good and strong tree and then
grafts it firmly within the weak tree. This in turn produces good
fruits, not from its own species but from the grafted species
of the strong tree. Similarly, our rotten nature produces good
fruits reaped from the acts of our Lord Jesus and the fruits of
His Holy Spirit".

Let us aim constantly to abide in Christ and His love, lest the
sin of death separate us from Him: "I am the vine, you are
the branches. He who abides in Me, and I in him, bears much
fruit" (Jn.15:5 NKJV). We abide in the grace of the Father, who
bestowed upon us His Son's body as a real symbol of abiding
in Him.

The Eucharist—The power of His Resurrection and participation in His suffering

Our Lord offered His body and blood on Thursday, when He
was seated among the disciples. Thus, when we participate
in the Liturgy, we profess the truth of our participation in the
death of our living Lord and His holy Resurrection. We partake
of His life-giving body, resurrected from the dead. We replace
the power of sin and death over the world with the power of
the Resurrection. We receive the life-giving body from the
life-giver, with the Priest saying: "For each time you eat of this
bread, and drink from this cup, you profess my death, declare
my resurrection and remember me until I return".

Then, the congregation responds in one voice, filled with the
power of the Resurrection: "Amen, Amen, Amen, we proclaim

your death O, Lord, and acknowledge your holy resurrection and your ascension to Heaven".

This very same partnership, which we practised during our baptism, is repeated each Liturgy, and each time we attend Liturgy, we proclaim before the Cross and before the empty tomb of Jesus. Each Liturgy is a Holy Passover, in which we cross over from death to life.

My Lord Jesus: I thank You because You bestowed upon me what Your disciples did not conceive at the time. You bestowed upon me the blessings of your cross and the mystery of knowing You. Make me worthy of the blessing from all these graces, not to neglect any of them. Do not allow my mind to be hindered nor deprived of conceiving these graces.

Within the mystery of the Last Supper, we see that the revelation of the mystery of the Resurrection is clearly included in the revelation of the mystery of His death. When Christ offers His body and blood to His disciples, saying, "Take My broken body, take and drink My shed blood", He offers the Eucharist—not as being dead, but as being alive in great power. In other words, in the mystery of the Last Supper, He was slain and resurrected simultaneously: at once dead and alive.

This is a mysterious sacrament whereby Christ reveals in full force the power of His Resurrection—an event that was inherently planned on His death on the Cross: "... I am the First and the Last. I am He who lives, and was dead, and behold, I am alive forevermore. Amen" (Rev. 1:17-18).

We can now understand the greatness of the Eucharist, which

Christ fulfilled on the Last Supper and which the Church continues to fulfil until today. This sacrament explains not only the mysteries of the Cross on Good Friday—it also explains the mysteries of the Resurrection. These mysteries include Christ's voluntary sacrifice of love and atonement for others on the Cross and the power of resurrecting others.

Based on the Eucharist, we are capable of receiving eternal life and remission of our past sins. This sacrifice holds for mankind an open partnership—one interwoven in Christ's body and blood, the slain and resurrected. The Church understands the concept that Christ's death on the cross was both a living and life-giving sacrifice, an atonement connected to resurrection. The Church understood all this through the mysteries of the Eucharist.

The Prayers and Readings of the Divine Liturgy

Since Sunday is the day of the Lord's Resurrection, the Church set a First Resurrection for the congregation throughout the year during Sunday liturgies. Many of the Sunday Matins Gospels speak of the women's visit to the tomb and the resurrection of Christ from the dead. The tune of: "This is the day the Lord has made; we will rejoice and be glad in it" is said during the Gospel of the Eve of the Feast of the Resurrection and every Sunday.

The ending of the litany of the Gospel incorporates the Resurrection: "Because You are the Life of us all, the Hope of us all, and the Resurrection of us all". This is said for every liturgy. The reconciliation prayer speaks of immortality following the coming of Christ (i.e., the Resurrection): "... and the death which came to the world, You have overcome through Your life-giving apparition". The reconciliation prayer also includes exchanging a holy kiss with one another, lest we become the subject of judgment. We have transferred from death to life through our love for one another:

"... and towards the end You came to us, who were seated in darkness and in in the shadows of death, You reached us through Your Only Son, our Lord, our God and our Saviour Jesus Christ, who blessed us with the divine birth from the water and Spirit (first resurrection); He purified us through His Holy Spirit, the Resurrection Spirit who resurrects our mortal bodies ... But if the Spirit of Him who raised Jesus from the dead dwells in you, He who raised Christ from the dead will also give life to your mortal bodies through His Spirit who dwells in you.

He who loved His own and submitted Himself to death which reigned over us in order to redeem us and He descended from the Cross to Hades (the place of the dead). He resurrected from among the dead, ascended to Heaven and sat on your right-hand (O Father).

Given for the forgiveness of sins and eternal life to all those who receive it. O Lord make us all worthy of receiving your Holies so we may become one body be worthy of a share and inheritance among all your saints."

This is connected to the First Resurrection.

In the final reconciliation, the Priest professes the truth of the First Resurrection to each person receiving Christ's body and blood: "This is the life-giving body of Your only Son, the only

One, given for us for salvation and for forgiveness of our sins and eternal life to whoever may receive it". Thus we see that the Divine Liturgy aims to enable a person to experience the reality of the power of the resurrection in our life through the Holy Eucharist.

The Resurrection in our Daily Life

The Resurrection removes failure and despair

Death amounts to the ultimate abyss of failure and despair in one's life. Therefore, it comes as no surprise that, in such a situation, one's life ends in the gutter of despair and failure. The Apostle Paul mentions that at one stage, he was so desperate—to the point of death—that he lost all confidence in himself. Then, he found comfort in the Resurrection:

"For we do not want you to be ignorant, brethren, of our trouble which came to us in Asia: that we were burdened beyond measure, above strength, so that we despaired even of life. Yes, we had the sentence of death in ourselves, that we should not trust in ourselves but in God who raises the dead, who delivered us from so great a death, and does deliver us; in whom we trust that He will still deliver us..." (2 Cor.1:8-10)

Paul experienced the first Resurrection when he despaired to the point of death and all doors seemed closed in front of him. In this moment, Paul turned to God. What person has not experienced despair at some point? People despair over issues regarding their finances, health, or spirituality. Any Christian will recall a time when they faltered in the face of their spiritual struggle to attain purity. Any Christian will recall a time when they found themselves at the threshold of mortal sin. Any Christian will recall a time when they failed to love, harbouring hatred instead. Then, suddenly, Jesus arrives through the closed doors in our life, saying, "Here I am", and shining love, courage, and hope on us.

What Christian has not reached that stage of hopelessness, only to be rescued by Jesus when they least expect it? "Therefore we do not lose heart. Even though our outward man is perishing, yet the inward man is being renewed day by day" (2 Corinthians 4:16-18). Saint Anthony the Great, for example, was an old man of 105 years. Outwardly, he appeared advanced in age and fragile, but spiritually he was at his prime. He never aged in a spiritual sense because he was renewed daily by his faith. With this example in mind, Christians should never fear failure—instead, we must step towards the First Resurrection and the realisation that we were raised with Jesus when the doors were shut.

As Christians, we must retain this hope when the doors to our future seem shut. When we place the entirety of our being in the Lord's hands, saying, "Your will be done, O Our Father who art in Heaven", we take comfort in the First Resurrection. In this moment, we are blessed with inner peace through the presence of God in our life. The Christian who endures physical suffering while reaping the gains of spiritual fulfilment joins the Apostle, saying, "For me, to live is Christ and to die is gain" (Philippians 1:21). At present, the Church is living the power of the Resurrection. This power triumphs over failure, despair and death.

The Resurrection triumphed over fear

Fear is the greatest enemy of the human being. The most intense fear is of fear itself. Fear sneaks into one's life through several means. Today, fear of the future is the dilemma of our younger generations. Many of our young people are fearful of their future, troubled by decisions to be made concerning academic, employment, and financial matters. Many parents are fearful of their children's future for the same reason.

Many mothers worry about the marriage prospects of their daughters—in some cases, resorting to witchcraft in a bid to secure their daughter's future. Many people are concerned over their future financial prospects: their income, expenses, and the type and location of their employment. These concerns about the future fall under the umbrella term of anxiety—of worrying about tomorrow even though tomorrow is in the hands of the Lord.

At the same time, many people experience fear that arises from looking to mistakes made in the past. Our concern over someone's negative opinion of us and deterioration in our relationships may lead us to repeat errors made in the past. In such moments, it is important to remember that our Lord Jesus came to His disciples through closed doors, wiping out all traces of their past.

Many among us are fearful of failure—a feeling that can arise from a lack of self-confidence. Fear of failure places doubt in a person's mind, leading them to question their ability to succeed in their desired field of endeavour. Illness is a familiar fear to many people. Often, unfounded fear of illness results in a phobia: hypochondriasis. When it comes to our physical health, Christians should remember that God has control of our physical bodies. Each and every one of our physical characteristics—even the number of hairs on our skin—are determined by God.

Some people are fearful of persecution, of facing oppression and false accusations. This fear is similar to our fear of stormy waves on a body of water, which often come suddenly and rock the boat we sit in—the boat that protects us from the water and the waves. When we feel this fear, Jesus responds by saying, "It is I. Don't be afraid".

Fear of death is the greatest fear of all. Often, I meet people whose fear of death increases with an advancing illness, with the fear continuing to escalate as a result of their concern over what will happen to their children in the future. Yet physicians remind patients constantly that psychological wellbeing is crucial if we are to cope with serious illness or advancing age. There are two types of reactions to the fear of death: one person receives peace and blessings of the Resurrection in their spirits, while the other becomes overwhelmed by fear, hastening their death in the process. Notably, fear of death is sometimes linked to the ego—our sense of our own self-importance.

How is it that some people no longer fear death? Consider the saints, who must have lived the Resurrection while crossing death. Some must have been in a state of rejoicing and said, "I desire to depart, which is much better". Others must have visualised death all their life, deciding to forsake the whole world as well as their ego. For some saints, death moved them to leave the world in order to worship in the desert. Saint Paul, for one, led his life striving to die. So, to answer the question I posed earlier, a person's fear of death remains until one's ego dies, and lives in the Resurrection.

1. The Triumphant First Resurrection is linked to the Cross

"Those who crucify the world for their souls, and their souls for the world, fear none: and those who do not covet and do not fear, have their feet on the summit of this world" Saint Augustine. The Lord told us many times to crucify the desires of the ego. He even clarified to what extent we should do this: "If anyone comes to me and does not hate father and mother, wife and children, brothers and sisters—yes, even their own life—such a person cannot be my disciple" (Luke 14:26). A person's ego may include their body and soul: "I tell you, my friends, do not be afraid of those who kill the body and after that have no more that they can do" (Luke 12:4). It may include selfishness concerning money, possessions, and status. Our Lord was poor in order to enrich us. He fled from Herod in order to allow us to retain our dignity. As Christians, we must remember that the ego is the root of fear.

2. The repentant do not fear death

Fear of death is caused by sin, and sin is the thorn of death. For these reasons, those who practise repentance and seek the salvation of their souls have no fear of death. They wait patiently to meet the Lord: "His Lord said to him, 'Well done, good and faithful servant; you have been faithful over a few things, I will make you ruler over many things. Enter into the joy of your Lord'".

3. The prayerful do not fear death

The saints teach us that the prayerful do not fear death. Prayer is the window through which we look towards eternity. Saints who spend their life in prayer live their eternity on Earth. Prayer amounts to striving towards constant presence with God; hence, the prayerful never fear death. I knew a woman whom I was with during her last moments. She kept pushing her hand under her pillow. For a moment, I thought perhaps she had her purse under the pillow. Then, I placed my hand next to hers under the pillow, but found that she had her Agpeya (Daily Prayer Book), which was with her all the time. Truly, where your treasure lies, your heart will be also. As Christians we should ask ourselves where we stand, in each moment, in comparison to those who had no fear about their ego (and on the contrary, they triumphed over their fear through prayer in the Resurrection). We should ask the Lord to bless us with the taste of the First Resurrection so that we may crucify the ego and lead a life of prayer in the Resurrection.

Icons of triumph over fear

1. The icon of the crucifixion of our Lord Jesus

Jesus had no concerns about His body. He was not fearful of the pain or shame of His crucifixion. He was not intimated by the wicked works of Herod, Pilate and the head Priests. Jesus loved everyone to the end. As a result, Jesus triumphed over the world: "In the world you will have tribulation; but be of good cheer, I have overcome the world" and, "... The prince of this world is coming. He has no hold over me". Jesus also triumphed over Satan and crushed him with the power of the Cross. He liberated the captives: "By which also he went and preached unto the spirits in prison" (1 Peter 3:19–20). He committed His spirit into His Father's hands ("into your hands I commit my spirit"), ascended into the Heavens, and drew all unto Him.

2. The icon of martyrs

The martyrs were filled with a power stronger than death—the power of the First Resurrection. Some of the martyrs died and were resurrected several times (for example, Saint George). Other martyrs rejected people's attempts to rescue them, instead joyfully opting for martyrdom. They understood that the power of the Resurrection was greater than the persecution they faced (for example, the 49 Elder Martyrs of Scetes). One powerful icon of martyrdom includes Saint Peter, the Seal of Martyrs. No soldier was capable of killing him. Each time an attempt was made, Peter's face shone with a heavenly light. Thus, the officer in charge of the execution offered 25 pieces of gold to whoever could sever Peter's neck. One person accepted the proposal and executed Peter with his sword.

Within the courage demonstrated by these martyrs, we can recognise the power of the Resurrection. Fear fled from them because they crucified their desires together with their bodies. They crucified themselves for the world. Martyrdom is the most significant power of the First Resurrection, and the power of resurrection is demonstrated in the struggle of the martyrs. Through the martyrs, the Church triumphed over governors who legislated to suppress Christians and their freedom. The Church ranks martyrs above saints because they are powerful witnesses of the First Resurrection.

3. Other pure icons
A promiscuous young woman was sent to Saint George to lure him into sin. When the young woman arrived, she found George praying. Immediately, her intention to seduce George was weakened—and to such an extent that the young woman ended up attaining the crown of martyrdom. She said, "They sent me to seduce you, but your purity drew me to salvation". This is the power of the Resurrection for a soul who is mortified towards the world, with Christ the immortal in it.

Another beautiful icon of purity is Joseph standing against the ruthless wife of Potiphar. Joseph knew the consequence of his rejection (either jail or death), yet he stood by his faith in the Resurrected God. The apostle Saint Paul described that one should do everything to strive against sin: "You have not yet resisted to bloodshed, striving against sin" (Hebrews 12:4). The pure icons will do this and have no fear in their life.

I have an unforgettable memory of a refugee, a young man who lived in Alexandria in a hotel owned by a divorcee. He described to me how the divorcee stood naked in front of him, trying to seduce him while also enticing him with money. The young man remained resolute in his morals, living the power of the Resurrection in the process.

4. Ascetics who do not worry about their bodies
Ascetics are devoted to fasting, showing no concern for the

weakness of their flesh. They spend nights in prayer without worrying about the weariness of their bodies. They renounce the world, saying, "'... and joyfully accepted the plundering of your goods, knowing that you have a better and an enduring possession for yourselves in heaven'. They rejoice when they are persecuted because of their Christ" (Hebrews 10:34-36). "'So, they departed from the presence of the council, rejoicing that they were counted worthy to suffer shame for His name'. Finally, they do not love their lives (Acts 5:41). "And they overcame him by the blood of the Lamb and by the word of their testimony, and they did not love their lives to the death" (Revelations 12:11).

In contrast, those who overstretch their bodies, fulfilling all their desires, suffer harm physically (such as obesity and heart problems) as well as spiritually. Christ arose and entered our lives through shut doors through our Baptisms. As Christians, we must cast away fear and strive to carry our cross with the One who crushed death by the power of death. To this end, we can rely on His golden promises:

- I am He, have no fear
- Do not fear those who kill the body
- Pray without ceasing.

5. An icon of the repentant has no fear of death
Although the Church is persecuted and suffering, her soul sings the anthem of the Resurrection:

"We are hard-pressed on every side, yet not crushed; we are perplexed, but not in despair; persecuted, but not forsaken; struck down, but not destroyed—always carrying about in the body the dying of the Lord Jesus, that the life of Jesus also may be manifested in our body. For we who live are always delivered to death for Jesus' sake, that the life of Jesus also may be manifested in our mortal flesh" (2 Corinthians 4:7-11).

When the fallen soul arises, it radiates a surge of power from the power of the Resurrection of the Lord Jesus.

The Resurrection of our mortal bodies

As Christians, the Resurrection impacted us spiritually and physically. It filled us with love, joy, and peace. As to our mortal bodies, the First Resurrection renewed our bodies into a life of purity and victory. The Resurrection within the concept of the Holy Bible is not confined only to the Final Resurrection (that is, when we rise from our graves). It includes the resurrected power that dwells within us: "But if the Spirit of Him who raised Jesus from the dead dwells in you, He who raised Christ from the dead will also give life to your mortal bodies through His Spirit who dwells in you" (Romans 8:11).

When Saint Paul cried: "O wretched man that I am! Who will deliver me from this body of death? I thank God—through Jesus Christ our Lord!" (Romans 7:24-25), he was aware that the Holy Spirit who dwelled in him was the one of the Resurrection. Through the Chrism, we become the temple of the Lord. Saint Paul emphasises this point in his epistle to the Corinthians: "Do you not know that your bodies are members of Christ? Shall I then take the members of Christ and make them members of a harlot? Certainly not!" (1 Corinthians 6:15). This means that the Lord Jesus became incarnate in our body: "and the Word became flesh and dwelt among us". Therefore, our bodies are not for adultery—they are for the Lord.

Our Lord took our bodies in order to give us life, in which He manifested His miraculous Resurrection. The Apostle says, "The Lord is in flesh". This means that He came for the salvation of our bodies through the power of the resurrection of His Body, of which we are members. Our physical bodies are blemished: full of lustful desires, motivated by the hunger of our egos. However, when our Lord was incarnate, He had an unblemished body from our pure Mother—Virgin Mary. He was raised and ascended to Heaven at the right hand of the Father with His glorified pure body. Consequently, we should detach our own bodies from earthly desires such as adultery, attaching ourselves only to the Lord, who took our bodies.

Christ the Lord (who was resurrected) is the head of the Church. This means the Church is the body of Christ. This same Lord will raise us with His own power. This great power was bestowed on our bodies to be the fruit of the union with the Logos of God.

The Resurrection and Crucifixion of the Body
The First Resurrection, which we acquire through Baptism, mortifies our bodies: "... always carrying about in the body the dying of the Lord Jesus, that the life of Jesus also may be manifested in our body" (2 Corinthians 4:10). The crucifixion of bodily lust is the path towards the resurrection of the body with Christ, fulfilling the Apostle's statement: "And those who are Christ's have crucified the flesh with its passions and desires". This means that it is not I who lives, but the resurrected Christ within me.

When the Apostle says, "... always carrying about in the body the dying of the Lord Jesus, that the life of Jesus also may be manifested in our body", he emphasises that we ought to constantly practise the power of Christ's death on our behalf. Through the burial of Baptism, we acquire power against bodily lust. The Apostle reiterates the dying of the body, saying, "For Your sake we are killed all day long; We are accounted as sheep for the slaughter" (Romans 8:36-39) and "And why do we stand in jeopardy every hour?" (1 Corinthians 15:30).

The Apostle reaffirms that the body resurrected with Christ is clothed in Christ: "But put on the Lord Jesus Christ, and make no provision for the flesh, to fulfil its lusts" (Romans 13:14). As Christians, we should remember that we are clothed in the Lord. This is our "first Resurrection". For this reason, we must harbour no lustful intentions for our bodies or our senses. A profound discipline is required to control our senses, as they are our means of setting our bodies towards channels of desires.

Freedom is the fruit of the Resurrection

The Resurrection is liberating. In contrast, being in Hades is imprisoning. The Lord Jesus triumphed by descending into Hades to liberate the captives. He liberated the captives who were under the servitude of Satan. Saint Peter says, "... He went and preached to the spirits in prison..." Both Adam and Eve obeyed Satan with their own free will. They preferred the advice of the Serpent rather than God's commandment. In effect, they surrendered their lives to Satan, submitting to him in total obedience. In turn, Satan enslaved and deprived

Adam and Eve of their true freedom in God.

Satan is a ruthless master. He is the Master of those who are attached to this world and its lusts. He is a liar (indeed, he is the father of all liars), and his pathway leads to Hell. Our Lord Jesus gave His life so that we may live: "that whoever believes in Him should not perish but have eternal life. For God so loved the world that He gave His only begotten Son, that whoever believes in Him should not perish but have everlasting life. For God did not send His Son into the world to condemn the world, but that the world through Him might be saved" (John 3:15-17).

The Israelites who endured Pharaoh's slavery did not enjoy the taste of freedom until the lamb was slaughtered (symbolising Crucifixion) and they crossed the Red Sea (symbolising Baptism). They fled to the wilderness as God's free children: "Therefore, we were buried with Him through baptism into death that just as Christ was raised from the dead by the glory of the Father, even so we also should walk in newness of life" (Romans 6:4).

The sinful person who has passed away is buried in the grave, with his wrists and ankles tied. These ties represent the bonds of sin. Jesus, who was sinless, experienced these bonds of sin when He was tied to the pole and scourged. His wrists and ankles were also tied when He was placed in the tomb. Satan attempts to lure us in the same way that Jesus suffered for our sake. Satan bonds the souls of his prey with love of the world and its lusts. He fills the hearts of his victims with darkness. Only after he gains full control does he scourge their souls, rendering them helpless. The Church prays constantly for these bound souls, saying, "... because You are the One who releases the bound; You are the Hope of the desperate; You are the help of the helpless".

Consider the following bonds of Satan:

Bodily lust
So often, this bond is restraining, making one's life a dark tomb. The souls who go through this abysmal darkness, which covers the soul upon succumbing to lust, become dead even as they are still alive. Once life on this earth comes to an end, there is no return. Hence, the Holy Spirit says to the soul who elects to live in the darkness of the tomb: "You can't do anything by your own power. You need the Resurrected Lord to resurrect you, like Christ said, 'Lazarus, come forth'". The deceased person is incapable of untying themselves.

Visual lust
This bond ties us to the abyss of the grave. Our Lord Jesus revealed to us the extent of the power of this bond: "The lamp of the body is the eye. Therefore, when your eye is good, your whole body also is full of light. But when your eye is bad, your body also is full of darkness. Therefore, take heed that the light which is in you is not darkness. If then your whole body is full of light, having no part dark, the whole body will be full of light, as when the bright shining of a lamp gives you light" (Luke 11:34-36).

When our eye focuses on reflecting on the image of the crucified Lord Christ, His wounded body and the moment He committed His spirit, His voice echoes in our ear, saying:

"Lazarus, come forth". Then, the Church absolves a person of sin: "If you forgive the sins of any, they are forgiven them; if you retain the sins of any, they are retained" (John 20:23-25).

Resentment, jealousy, envy and hatred

These vicious bonds make the human heart dark and putrid. Often I encounter people who say, "I wish I could love everyone, but I can't". Experiencing the darkness of the tomb is awful. This happens when one is driven by the kind of lustful desires mentioned earlier. Hatred equals death, in contrast to love which is life: "We know that we have passed from death to life, because we love the brethren. He who does not love his brother abides in death" (1 John 3:13).

Arrogance and love of status

Arrogance is among the most dangerous bonds that lead to enslavement. The arrogant person is unreceptive to the Cross, which is the pathway to Resurrection. Instead, their main focus is their own ego, with no tolerance for any other behaviour. For them, the Cross is a stumbling block. Arrogance is the route to the fall; all its victims are mighty.

Reflect on what our Lord Jesus said: "Take My yoke upon you and learn from Me, for I am gentle and lowly in heart, and you will find rest for your souls". He carried His cross without resentment. He was insulted while He was God and He submitted Himself to death and burial. In this way, He broke free from the bonds of arrogance.

Love of the world

This is the strongest bond we have witnessed throughout the

twentieth century and up to now. Even within the Church, Satan exploits this bond, whether through love of food, of one's appearance, or of greed. Our Lord described Satan as "the ruler of this world". Those whose first love is of this world give Satan an open invitation to enter their heart, transferring their heart into lethal darkness in the process. Love of this world is death, and liberation from this world is a great resurrection.

Fear

This bond restrains us as human beings. The ultimate state of fear is excessive concern about one's body and soul. Our Lord Jesus liberated us from fear: "If anyone comes to Me and does not hate his father and mother, wife and children, brothers and sisters, yes, and his own life also, he cannot be My disciple" (Luke 14:26). Jesus also said that we should not fear those who kill the body. Those who live in fear are dead while being alive. Resurrection is liberty from the fear of death.

As Christians, we need to remove fear from our hearts—regardless of the situation. If, for example, we are imprisoned unfairly, or if we are treated harshly, or if we fall into the grips of suffering (whether emotional or physical), we should remove fear from our hearts.

Oh my soul, how often did you cross the valley of the shadow of death, nevertheless your Lord freed you. He blessed you, Oh my soul, with the first Resurrection. Oh My Lord, I join Saint Augustine when you free me from the bonds of lust, fear, and arrogance. I join him saying, "I placed my feet on the summit of this world when I became fearless of anything and when I ceased to desire anything".

The Cross: the path to the Resurrection (and to freedom)

On the Feast of the Cross, the Church reads Saint John's Gospel (8:31, 36): "If you abide in My word, you are My disciples indeed. And you shall know the truth, and the truth shall make you free" and, "Therefore, if the Son makes you free, you shall be free indeed". During the Vespers of the third Sunday, following the Resurrection, the same Gospel is read. In addition, the Gospel of the liturgy of the third Sunday teaches the practical side of freedom, recounting Jesus' meeting with the Samaritan woman who was enslaved to sin. Our Lord Jesus liberated and raised this woman.

The Church links the Feast of the Cross to the Feast of the Resurrection in both of its readings: "Therefore, if the Son makes you free, you shall be free indeed". This verse is also read on the same day of the account of the Samaritan woman. As a live icon of the Cross, she symbolises freedom and resurrection from lust and hypocrisy. No one can taste the Resurrection without carrying the Cross. The Cross is our path to freedom from the chains of the world and its lusts: "But God forbid that I should boast except in the cross of our Lord Jesus Christ, by whom the world has been crucified to me, and I to the world" (Galatians 6:14) and, "And those who are Christ's have crucified the flesh with its passions and desires" (Galatians 5:24).

As for those who struggle against sin until death, they are the ones who achieve freedom and the first Resurrection. For this reason, our Lord placed a condition on those who wish to be His disciples. He required them to carry their cross and deny themselves in order to attain freedom in Christ. As Christians, we cannot live the Resurrection without carrying the teachings of the Gospel. To think otherwise—that the first Resurrection is achievable without practising the Gospel teachings—is an illusion.

Resurrection and Freedom

If you were asked to paint an icon for freedom, how would you choose to portray it? Perhaps as a bird flying from a cage? A bird living in a cage is kept safe; a bird living in a cage has food—but can it have true freedom? Our Church's icon for freedom is a profound one.

The Icon of Resurrection is the Icon of Freedom

Christ was in a dark tomb, His wrists and ankles bound. A huge stone was mounted on top of His tomb. The tomb was blocked with the Governor's seal and secured by armed guards. Even so, Christ arose from His tomb triumphant, symbolising the most magnificent icon of freedom.

The Icon of the Martyr

The greatest depiction of an icon for a martyr is that of John the Baptist, who is portrayed holding his severed head on his hand, even before it was cut off by Herod. The most magnificent images of freedom and Resurrection are those of people who overcome their ego and desires with their spirits, soaring into heaven in the power of the Resurrection even as they remain alive in their earthly bodies. The spirits of the martyrs soared from their bodies before being killed by Governors. Thus, the martyrs marched forward joyfully and bravely. It is for this reason that we honour the martyrs as a living model of freedom.

The Icon of Repentance

A sinner is a slave to Satan. He may be enslaved to the desires of the world, being filled with resentment and hatred. Darkness fills the sinner's heart, making them anxious over the future.

1. The Prodigal Son

The Prodigal Son regarded his father's home as a prison and a place of servitude. In the son's view, the servants in his father's home were happier than him. At the end of each day, they left the father's home and squandered their wages on extravagances and indulgences. The Prodigal Son felt restricted by his father's instructions and domestic commitments. He may have thought that his father's house was nothing but a workplace—that he would be able to access real freedom by leaving his father's house. Thus, he left his father's house and fell in the trap of Satan, reaching a state close to death. Therefore, when the Prodigal Son returned to his father's house, his father said, "He was dead (chained) and now he is alive (raised and free)". In other words, the son was dead until he arose through the first Resurrection, and finally could enjoy true freedom.

The Prodigal son viewed the first Baptism and his life with

Jesus as restrictive. However, after his repentance, he saw this way of living bestowed freedom from the slavery of the enemy. In the past, he had viewed eating a fattened calf at his Father's home as a normal meal—one attached to many restrictions. Now, he viewed the sacrifices made by his Father as the Lord's meal, representing His body, which raises men from death.

For the Prodigal Son, his Father's commandments—which had seemed imprisoning—were now tied to love and kisses in his Father's bosom. In fact, slavery is living under the chains of lust. Freedom (that is, Resurrection) is life in the bosom of the Father. The Father's commandments are not burdensome but are like a cross. The Cross amounts to fulfilling the commandments that are the pathway to freedom, the fruit of the first Resurrection with Christ.

2. The Samaritan Woman

This is the Gospel of the third Sunday of the Holy Fifty days. In this Gospel, it seems that the Church wants to lay before us a practical example of freedom and First Resurrection on the third Sunday. The Church does this through the story of the Samaritan Woman. The Samaritan woman was a slave to five husbands, bound by lust and resentment. Our Lord released and liberated her from her chains through her repentance and confession.

Consider that the effort exerted by the Lord to resurrect the Samaritan Woman was far greater than what He exerted to resurrect Lazarus. The Lord's raising of Lazarus involved a single sentence: "Lazarus, come out". In contrast, raising the Samaritan woman required Him to walk for an entire day, standing in the noon heat at the well, thirsting for water, humbling Himself before the woman, and engaging in a long sophisticated discussion with her. Loosening the ties of the Samaritan woman was harder than raising Lazarus.

The Freedom and the First Resurrection are our Lord's intention for Earth's chained souls. Today, so many young people are chained to their desires, and so many adults are chained to coveting and attaching to the world. We should remember that our Lord Jesus came with His message:

- "To proclaim liberty to the captives"
- "To set at liberty those who are oppressed" (Luke 4:18)
- "... If the Son makes you free, you shall be free indeed" (John 8:36).

This is our Lord's message. It is His call for us to taste the sweetness of freedom and the First Resurrection, like the Samaritan Woman who put her feet on the summit of this world (in line with what Saint Augustine had said) when she lost her lust for men and her fear of other people gossiping about her.

The Icon of Freedom: An Icon of Praise

An icon of the soul enjoys freedom even as they remain imprisoned in their body. An icon of the soul is a soul who is liberated from the chains of the world and of lust, a soul who flies in the heavens, sharing existence with God. An icon of the soul lives within the body, but is in constant and loving dialogue with Christ. The best example of an icon of the soul is found in Saint Augustine's confessions. Following his return from a life spent in evil, Saint Augustine had a conversation with his mother, Monica:

"Both of us used to yearn within ourselves to that divine spring which overflowed with life. When we reached that state of harmony, this earnest wish diminished all other joys with all their lures until they became so trivial not worth comparison or even mention next to your happiness. We flew with a flamed desire towards God. Through our flight we passed through layers and layers of the materialistic world up to the majestic Heavens with its sun, its moon and the stars which we passed through without any effort. Within ourselves, we felt an intangible loftiness, until we reached this infinity where you are seated O [God] feeding the righteous of the food of the truth for ever."

The Apostle Saint Paul calls upon us as Christians to "Stand fast therefore in the liberty by which Christ has made us free, and do not be entangled again with a yoke of bondage" (Galatians 5:1). With this in mind, we can choose to stand fast in his liberty. Its cost is the precious blood of Christ, who liberated us from Satan's bondage, from the world, and the body. Freedom is a divine Grace. In this way, it is like the Resurrection, whereby Christ entered our lives, our minds, and our souls through closed doors. He filled us with worship and praise.

Procession of the Light

The procession of the light is the procession for the Resurrection by the Children of the Light and Resurrection. The associated Gospel, the Fourth Sunday of the Pentecostal Period, describes the First Resurrection as a procession by the children of the light, who walk in the light of the Resurrection of our Lord Jesus in a world living in darkness:

- "Walk while you have the light, lest darkness overtake you; he who walks in darkness does not know where he is going. While you have the light, believe in the light, that you may become sons of light" (John 12:35).

- "I have come as a light into the world, that whoever believes in Me should not abide in darkness" (John 12:46).

- "I am the light of the world. He who follows Me shall not walk in darkness but have the light of life" (John 8:12).

We lived in the darkness of death in the tomb. Our Lord arose to shine His Light upon those who lived in darkness and the shadows of death (the Divine Liturgy). The Apostle draws links between the light that shone at the creation of the old world ("Let there be light") and the Light that shone at the glorious Resurrection—"And the Light shines in the darkness, and the darkness did not comprehend it" (John 1:5).

For it is the God who commanded light to shine out of darkness, who has shone in our hearts to give the light of the knowledge of the glory of God in the face of Jesus Christ (2 Corinthians 4:6).

The acts of Light are acts of God. Thus, as Christians, we are called "Children of the Light". Saint Paul explains: "For you were once darkness, but now you are light in the Lord. Walk as children of Light ..." (Ephesians 5:8-11). "... He who does the truth comes to the light, that his deeds may be clearly seen, that they have been done in God" (John 3:21). The First Resurrection was a combination of behaviour and deeds.

Before Christ, life was darkness controlled by Satan: "You are of your father the devil, and the desires of your father you want to do" (John 8:44).

In contrast, life in Christ, the Resurrected from the dead, is wholly acts of God: "For you were once darkness, but now you are light in the Lord. Walk as children of light (for the fruit of the Spirit is in all goodness, righteousness, and truth), finding out what is acceptable to the Lord. And have no fellowship with the unfruitful works of darkness, but rather expose them" (Ephesians 5:8-11).

The Apostle affirms that those who do the works of the Light will arise from the dead and lead a serious life, because they lived in death in the past: "Awake, you who sleep, Arise from the dead, And Christ will give you light" (Ephesians 5:14). Sin is the work of Satan, of darkness, and death. Death is existence within the walls of a tomb. Christian behaviour, however, is the procession of the children of light, whereby their hearts are filled of the light of Christ's Resurrection.

The Light of Deeds

Resurrection amounts to following the teachings of the Holy Spirit, which God had laid down: "He who comes from above is above all; he who is of the earth is earthly and speaks of the earth. He who comes from heaven is above all" (John 3:31). The works of the flesh are those of the children of darkness: "Now the works of the flesh are evident, which are: adultery, fornication, uncleanness, lewdness, idolatry, sorcery, hatred, contentions, jealousies, outbursts of wrath, selfish ambitions, dissensions, heresies, envy, murders, drunkenness, revelries, and the like; of which I tell you beforehand, just as I also told you in time past, that those who practice such things will not inherit the kingdom of God" (Galatians 5:19-21).

The works of the flesh are conducted by the children of Satan: "You belong to your father, the devil, and you want to carry out your father's desires" (John 8:44). In contrast, the works of the Light are conducted by the children of the Resurrection: "Let your light so shine before men, that they may see your good works and glorify your Father in heaven" (Matthew 5:16). These are the fruits of the Holy Spirit: "But the fruit of the Spirit is love, joy, peace, longsuffering, kindness, goodness, faithfulness, gentleness, self-control" (Galatians 5:22).

The Light of the Truth

Christ is the Truth and Christ is the Light of the world. Whoever receives the Truth comes to the Light. God's work will be manifested in these people in the light of the First Resurrection. Those who establish their life and their works based on lies are the children of Satan: the father of liars. They follow him through the procession of darkness to death: "You are of your father the devil. When he speaks a lie, he speaks from his own resources, for he is a liar and the father of it" (John 8:44).

The Light of the Eye

"The lamp of the body is the eye. If therefore your eye is good, your whole body will be full of light. But if your eye is bad, your whole body will be full of darkness" (Matthew 6:22-23). When the eye shines, it does so upon the whole body, making us children of the First Resurrection and children of the Light. In contrast, when dimmed, the eye can place our entire body in darkness and in a tomb in which death dwells.

The Light of the Cross

The Cross is the Light of the Resurrection. Our holy Church describes the Cross as: "The Holy wood on which our Lord was kindled, and He shined upon our life" (Feast of the Cross Prayer). A person without partnership with the Cross is like a lighthouse without a beacon. Thus, those who share our Lord's Cross rejoice in the light of His Resurrection. The crucifixion of the body, with its desires and lust, bursts into the soul the joys of the Resurrection and its light. The opposite is also true: it is impossible for a soul to rejoice in the light of the Resurrection without partnership with our Saviour's Cross.

The Light of the Mind

"Let this mind be in you, which was also in Christ Jesus" (Phil 2:5-11). The Light of the Mind is the humble, simple, and contrite mind. Whoever follows Christ's thought lives and rejoices in the Light of the Resurrection.

The Light of God's Mind and Prayers

"Your word is a lamp to my feet. And a light to my path" (Psalms 119:105). "It gives understanding to the simple" (Psalms .119:130). Prayers made Moses' face shine, so that even his people could not gaze at him. The Transfiguration reflected Christ's light on the faces of Moses and Elijah when the Lord took His disciples up the mountain for prayer. His face was lit up like the sun, because it is "Through your Light O Lord, we see the Light". Each time we stand before Christ for prayer, we walk up the loftiness of our God's Light and His Resurrection.

The Light of Love

"He who loves his brother abides in the light" (1 John 2:10). Love is walking in the Light. The Apostle also links the First Resurrection to love: "We know that we have passed from death to life, because we love the brethren" (1 John 3:14-15).

Therefore, on the first day of the Pentecostal Period, we should remember to ask ourselves: are we behaving like those who walk in the procession of the light as children of the light? Are we firm in the Truth, and at the same time maintaining love? Are we leading a life of purity? Are our hearts full of peace? In other words: is the whole of our life soaked in light—our bodies, our souls, and our deeds? Have the deeds of darkness fled from our life after our Resurrection with Christ and our walking in the Light?

The works of darkness extinguish the flame of the soul, filling the heart with grudges, hatred, impurity, ego-feeding human glory, and worldly lust—all of which end in death. So, as Christians, our Lord Jesus, Light of the world, the Resurrected from among the dead, calls upon us: "Walk in the Light, so that you become Children of the Light. Work the works of the Light so that the works of darkness and death flee from your life; thus, becoming truly the children of the First Resurrection which is not subject to the authority of the second death".

The First Resurrection and hidden life with Christ

"For you died, and your life is hidden with Christ in God... that just as Christ was raised from the dead by the glory of the Father, even so we also should walk in newness of life" (Romans 6:4-5). Our Resurrection is the fruit of our union with the resurrected Christ and Glory is our share in the glorified and resurrected Christ. Thus, the hidden life with Christ is the only way to Resurrection and Glory. The feast of Resurrection is completely joined with our hidden life with Christ.

Our life became hidden with Christ in God during Baptism. We were buried with Him: "For if we have been united together in the likeness of His death, certainly we also shall be in the likeness of His resurrection" (Romans 6:4-5). Through Baptism, we are now living the Resurrection, because our life is hidden with Christ in God. Through the Holy Spirit (Chrism ointment), the Spirit of Christ dwells within us, our life hid in Him, and our bodies savoured the sweetness of the Resurrection.

But if the Spirit of Him who raised Jesus from the dead dwells in you, He who raised Christ from the dead will also give life to your mortal bodies through His Spirit who dwells in you. (Romans 8:11)

Spiritual warfare and repentance: Resurrection with Christ
The spirits who are hidden with Christ put to death their sins daily, because Christ who is our life is resurrected: "... but if by the Spirit you put to death the deeds of the body, you will live ... if indeed we suffer with Him, that we may also be glorified together" (Romans 8:13-17). Resurrection with Christ is linked to our death with Him: as Christians, we died and our lives are hidden with Christ. With this in mind, we should taste death at each moment, away from the world and away from sin.

Therefore put to death your members which are on the earth: fornication, uncleanness, passion, evil desire, and covetousness, which is idolatry....But now you yourselves are to put off all these: anger, wrath, malice, blasphemy...and have put on the new man who is renewed in knowledge according to the image of Him who created him... since you have put off the old man with his deeds. (Colossians 3:5-10)

Only those whose life is hidden with Christ on His cross, and who cast away their old being with its deeds, will taste the Resurrection and its joys.

The essence of the Resurrection is seeking things that are above

By the same token, Christians whose life is hidden with the Resurrected Christ experience the feelings as the Resurrected Christ:"... seek those things which are above, where Christ is, sitting at the right hand of God ... set your mind on things above, not on things on the earth" (Colossians 3:1-2). We have no life other than that with Christ. With Him, we are clothed in the new image—one that is generated towards knowledge according to the image of its Creator. "... where there is neither Greek nor Jew, circumcised nor uncircumcised, barbarian, Scythian, slave nor free, but Christ is all and in all" (Colossians 3:11).

Receiving the Lord's Body is being hidden in the Resurrection

Enlightenment with Christ in God leads us to resoluteness in the Resurrected Christ in the sacrament of the Eucharist: "He who eats My flesh and drinks My blood abides in Me, and I in him" (John 6:56). The Communion of the Lord's Body is the share of the repentant souls, resurrected with Christ. What we receive is the Bread from Heaven. Whoever eats from it shall not die, but will live the Resurrection for eternity. "If anyone eats of this bread, he will live forever; and the bread that I shall give is My flesh, which I shall give for the life of the world" (John 6:55-56).

As Christians, we are the resurrected Church that sits above death and the whole world. On this basis, we can rejoice, knowing that we are alive in our Baptism and the Holy Spirit who dwells in us through the power of the Resurrection. We can rejoice that we are leading lives of repentance, casting away the old, seeking what is above, and living the joys of the Resurrection. We are partaking in the Lord's Body and Blood, and thus living the happy eternity with God.

Evangelising the Resurrection

Evangelism was the first mission following the Resurrection. That said, it was understood that Evangelists should have witnessed the Resurrection. How could a person who doubted the Resurrection proclaim that the One who was placed in the tomb was resurrected, arriving through closed doors? How could that person evangelise to sinners about the Lord's ability to raise the fallen? How could they evangelise to captives about freedom?

For this reason, evangelism had to go through two stages. The first was the pre-Pentecost, which is the period when the Lord focused on resurrecting the Disciples, giving them the authority to evangelise to those who were to be raised. The second stage was the post-Pentecost. In that period, the Lord remained with the Disciples for forty days.

Principles of Evangelism

The Evangelist who experiences the power of the Resurrection (which covers Baptism, Repentance, and Holy Communion with Christ through the Holy Spirit) is accountable in the first degree in their role as Evangelist. It was only after the Disciples had experienced the First Resurrection that they evangelised. Otherwise, they would have been regarded as frauds. Thus, the first prerequisite for the selection of the Apostle Matthias in lieu of Judas was that "... this Scripture had to be fulfilled, which the Holy Spirit spoke before by the mouth of David concerning Judas ..." (Acts 1:16).

"And they prayed and said, 'You, O Lord, who know the hearts of all, show which of these two You have chosen to take part in this ministry and apostleship from which Judas by transgression fell, that he might go to his own place'. And they cast their lots, and the lot fell on Matthias. And he was numbered with the eleven apostles" (Acts 1:23-26).

The Lord appeared to Thomas for all to see the Resurrection and cast away all shadows of doubt, fear and cowardice. Once the Resurrection surged its power in them, Peter became brave, Thomas believed, and the rest of the apostles rejoiced. The Holy Spirit descended upon them on Pentecost and they became an Evangelical power throughout the world.

The Resurrected Church: an Evangelical power

After the Resurrection, the State of the Disciples is the most magnificent image of the power of the Evangelist Church. It is an image that includes Christ's tomb—the seals, the guards, the evil priests—along with a group of eleven apostles inside an upper room, dying of fear, behind closed doors. Then, suddenly, we see that Christ has risen from the dead, and the images are reversed. Instead, the guards and soldiers look as though they are dying from fear, the evil Head Priests are in an extreme state of confusion, and the once-weak Apostles are in the climax of rejoicing and peace.

This image is the Resurrected Church. Without swords and without weaponry, but nonetheless "awesome like an army with banners" (Song of Songs 6:4) in the face of the Roman Rule and the repression of the Jews. It is the Church evangelising joy, courage and peace, with the government and Jews standing in great fear in response.

At this point, fear moved from the Resurrected Church, evangelising in the name of the crucified Jesus of Nazareth, and set upon the defeated enemy and the fearful ruler. The Book of Acts describes repeatedly the joy, strength, and courage that filled the hearts of the disciples—and remember, the disciples were simple in terms of education, they were few in number, and they were unarmed, except for the power of the Resurrection. "They continued to meet in the temple courts. They broke bread in their homes and ate together with glad and sincere hearts" (Acts 2:46). Most miraculous was the fact that the young man who stoned Stephen became a co-preacher with the disciples: "The man who formerly persecuted us is now preaching the faith he once tried to destroy" (Galatians 1:23).

Evangelism: A prime commitment to resurrected souls
The prime commitment entrusted by The Lord to Mary

Magdalene, after she witnessed His Resurrection, kneeling before Him and touching His feet, was to evangelise to the disciples and not waste time. Evangelism was the prime commitment entrusted to whoever saw and felt the Resurrection: "Then go quickly ..." (Matthew 28:7) "... Go and tell my brothers to go to Galilee; there they will see me" (Matthew 28:10).

The Disciples witnessed His Resurrection and were resurrected with Him away from sin and fear. The Lord's commitment to the Disciples was: "Therefore go and make disciples of all nations, baptising them in the name of the Father and of the Son and of the Holy Spirit" (Matthew 28:19). The Lord affirmed that Evangelism was an extension of His own Evangelism: "'Peace be with you! As the Father has sent me, I am sending you'. And with that he breathed on them and said, 'Receive the Holy Spirit...'" (John 20:21-22).

He made an emphatic commandment to Saint Peter, which He repeated three times and summed up in a vital equation: there is no love of Christ without Evangelism. This was demonstrated in his call: "'Simon, son of Jonah, do you love Me more than these?' He said to Him, 'Yes, Lord; You know that I love You'. He said to him, 'Feed My lambs'. He said to him again a second time, 'Simon, son of Jonah, do you love Me?' He said to Him, 'Yes, Lord; You know that I love You'. He said to him, 'Tend My sheep'. He said to him the third time, 'Simon, son of Jonah, do you love Me?' Peter was grieved because He said to him the third time, 'Do you love Me?' And he said to Him, 'Lord, You know all things; You know that I love You'. Jesus said to him, 'Feed My sheep'" (John 21:15-17).

This is a clear call upon those resurrected with Christ, whereby they are transferred from the cowardly Peter to Peter the Evangelist of 3,000—Peter the witness of the Resurrection, fearless and with such great love that he was crucified and died for His sake. Serving and pastoring is a clear demonstration of the love of resurrected souls.

The time of the Resurrection: the great season for fishing

He met them while they were fishing and upon His giving them authority, they got out 153 large fish (John 9:11). This is the calibre of service and evangelism that followed the Resurrection: the fish were large in size and plentiful in number. He had told them: "I shall make you fishermen of people". After the Resurrection and during the Pentecostal period, the Church focused on the fishing and the ministry. At the vespers of the second Wednesday, the Gospel on the Harvest is read: "He told them, 'The harvest is plentiful, but the workers are few. Ask the Lord of the harvest, therefore, to send out workers into his harvest'" (Luke 10:2).

At the Vespers of the Saturday of the second week, the Church speaks to us about the catching of fish (Luke 5:2-10) and how our Lord transferred Peter from a fisherman to a fisherman of people. This came after Peter's repentance, admission of his sin, and witnessing of the Resurrection.

As Christians, we should remember:

- Pentecost is the start of the Fishing Season.
- The power of fishing is attached to the power of Resurrection.

- Evangelism is the mission of those who experience the Resurrection.

- There is no Evangelism without Resurrection.

- Ministry and pastorship represent the love of Christ.

- Evangelism is the extension of the Son's mission delegated by His Father.

The Cross and the Resurrection in the life of Saint Mary

Firstly, we should consider the role of the Cross in the life of Saint Mary. The Virgin shared the Lord Jesus' life on earth. To begin with, she conceived Him for nine months. As she suffered labour pains, she had to travel and delivered Him in a manger. Later, she fled to Egypt through the barren desert. She stood next to Him near the Cross.

Simeon the Elder said of Saint Mary: "... and said to His mother Mary: 'Yes, a sword will pierce through your heart'" (Luke 2:35). The Church speaks of Mary's emotions in the section of the ninth hour prayers: "The world rejoices in receiving salvation, but my heart burns when I watch your crucifixion which You are stoically enduring for the sake of all, O my Son and my God".

Blessed are you O our Mother, O Mother of the whole of humankind. You delivered from your womb on our behalf God's Word Incarnate. You represented us in enduring all those sufferings and the pain of that sword.

Secondly, we should consider the Resurrection in our lives. Some Eastern Churches believe that the Virgin Mary did not go to the tomb for the Resurrection, but that the Angel visited her to announce the glorious Resurrection. The Virgin Mary was the partner of all of humankind in the joys of the Resurrection. She attained the first Resurrection of humankind before anyone else. She also knew the mystery of incarnation before anyone else.

The Virgin also knew how Christ the Lord left her womb: she delivered Him while all the doors were shut, in fulfilment of Ezekiel's prophecy. "This gate shall be shut, it shall not be opened, and no man shall enter in by it" (Ezekial44:2). This was the same mystery, down to the smallest detail, as our Lord's exit from the tomb: He resurrected, and the stone remained as it was and the seals were unbroken.

O Virgin, who on this earth is like you to fathom this mystery of your perpetual virginity? No doubt, it is the same mystery of the sealed tomb from which the Lord was raised.

The angels received infant Jesus with praise and evangelised the message to the Shepherds. Similarly, both angels received the news of the Resurrection and evangelised the message to the Marys.

O Virgin Mother: the entry and the leaving of our Lord when he visited the Disciples in the upper room, while doors were shut, is the very mystery of His being in your womb and the doors being shut.

Blessed art You, O Mother, because you are the only one blessed with the mysteries of His incarnation, the mystery of His Resurrection within you only, the mystery of your virginity, the mysteries of Resurrection with shut doors. All these divine mysteries will be revealed to us who are of your own race and for us to experience them in life, each day, each moment even though all doors are shut.

God loved the world, sent His Word, and became incarnate of the Virgin Mary. Jesus carried our sins, was crucified on our behalf, forgave us our sins, and was resurrected with our body, which He took of our Lady. Thus, He resurrected us with Him.

Consider this: was our First Resurrection with Him the sole aim of His incarnation journey? The answer is no: had the Resurrection been the only aim of the journey, our share would have been to remain with Him eternally on this earth. God's aim was to raise the Church (in His own body), seat her at the right hand of the Father, and give her the Holy Spirit: the Father's Spirit (the Father's Promise). This was the aim of the beginning and end of Christ's journey on Earth: "I go to prepare a place for you" (John 14:2).

What is the meaning of this whole statement: What is this place? Is it a tangible one? "And if I go and prepare a place for you, I will come back and take you to be with me that you also may be where I am"(John 14:3) Is the intended meaning that after we die, He will take us to live with Him for ever? "For if we believe that Jesus died and rose again, even so God will bring with Him those who sleep in Jesus" (Thessalonians 4:15).

Our Lord Jesus took the body from our Virgin Lady: in other words, a human body. He raised us up with this body and we became members of His own body. He ascended with this body and was seated at the right hand of the Father—that is, He seated us at the right hand of the Father. However, the

Father is spirit, He has no right hand. So, where did He seat us?

When He ascended with the Church (His body) to Heaven, He revealed to us a serious fact and an eternal place: God is Father and we (the Church, body of Christ) were placed in the bosom of the Father. This is not a physical bosom—it is a factual proclamation that God is our Father; this is the place Christ had prepared for us and where He took us with Him. Next time you worship, consider that you (and the entire Church around you) is seated at the right hand of the Father and is living in His bosom. Physically, we are living on earth; we lead a life of being Christ's children, within the Father's bosom. As you sit at the right hand of the Father, remember: you have a Heavenly Father who watches over you. "My prayer is not that you take them out of the world but that you protect them from the evil one" (John 17:15).

We sit at the right hand of the Father whether we are on Earth or in the hereafter. From the moment Christ ascended to Heaven and was seated at the right hand of the Father, we were in the bosom of the Father with Him. There is no relation between this existence and our physical existence on Earth or our departure to Heaven. What separates us from the bosom of the Father is the evil one. That is why our Lord said: "My prayer is not that you take them out of the world but that you protect them from the evil one" (John 17:15).

<u>"I will not leave you as orphans" (John 14:18)</u>
An orphan is a child without a father or mother. Christ calls the orphan world to be a member of His body: that is, He calls

the Church to have a place at the right hand of the Father, where Christ is seated. The world is called to be in Christ, in life within the Fatherhood of Christ, instead of in life as orphans.

"I am the Way and the Truth and the Life. No one comes to the Father except through me" (John 14:6).

This is not a way in the sense that it is physically drawn on a map. No one knows God as a Father unless one is seated at His right hand, and no one is seated at His right hand except His Son, Jesus Christ, and we the members of His body. This is the meaning of the Way: being steadfast in Christ leads us to the right hand of the Father. This is why Christ the Lord kept repeating, in several verses:

- "Remain in me, as I also remain in you... Neither can you bear fruit unless you remain in me" (John 15:4).

- "As the Father has loved me, so have I loved you. Now remain in my love" (John 15:9).

- "And I will do whatever you ask in my name, so that the Father may be glorified in the Son" (John 14:13).

- "A little while longer and the world will see Me no more" (John 14:19).

We are members of His body: when we seek and we receive, we become good members of the Body of the Son. People will watch our good deeds, glorifying the Father because of us: the members of the Body of the Son. Thus, the Father is glorified through the Son. The world does not see Him because He is not physically among us, but we see Him even more so, because we are His children, and His Spirit dwells within us. He shows Himself to the members of His body: "Thomas said to him, 'Lord, we don't know where you are going, so how can we know the way?' Jesus answered, 'I am the Way and the Truth and the Life. No one comes to the Father except through me. If you really know me, you will know my Father as well. From now on, you do know him and have seen him'" (John 14:5).

Whoever remains steadfast in Him becomes a firm member—not merely seeing Him, but feeling Him: "Anyone who loves me will obey my teaching. My Father will love them, and we will come to them and make our home with them" (John 14:23).

<u>"If you loved Me, you would be glad that I am going to the Father, for the Father is greater than I" (John 14:28).</u>
Whoever loves Christ would also love for Christ to fulfil His mission, seating the whole Church at the right hand of the Father in the process. However, Christians who are ignorant of those facts might feel saddened, God forbid, believing Christ left the world in His body without fulfilling His mission. Consequently, He would not have led the Church to the bosom of the Father, which is greater than Christ remaining with us on Earth.

For this reason, He said, "You are in Me, in the bosom of the Father, which is greater than being among you on Earth in this body". The Father's bosom is greater than the whole Earth: that is, the Father is greater than Him while He is with us on Earth.

"So that the world may learn that I love the Father and do exactly what my Father has commanded me. 'Come now; let us leave" (John 14:31).

The love of the Father calls us to leave the world: its conflicts, its commitments, its concerns. If, as Christians, we sit at the right hand of the Father, then we should get going spiritually, moving away from the worries of the world. All the while, we should proclaim our love of the Father, since we are seated at His right hand.

"Remain in me, as I also remain in you." (John 15:4).

"Our existence at the right hand of the Father is part of being steadfast in Christ. Without it, we are not the Father's children because He is the only One seated at the right hand of the Father" (John 15:4).

"Now remain in my love" (John 15:9).

"God is Love. Whoever is steadfast in God is to remain steadfast in Love. Love of all. For this reason, He repeated, 'My command is this: Love each other as I have loved you'" (John 15:12, 17).

"... and I do not say to you that I shall pray the Father for you; for the Father Himself loves you" (John 16:26-27).

So, reader: since you love Christ, you are now a member of His body. He seats you at the right hand of the Father with Him. Therefore, whatever is the Father's is also the Son's— consequently, that applies to all members of His body also. The Father Himself loves us because we are His children and He is our Father.

"... but I will see you again and you will rejoice... In that day you will no longer ask me anything. Very truly I tell you, my Father will give you whatever you ask in my name. Until now you have not asked for anything in my name. Ask and you will receive, and your joy will be complete" (John 16-24).

Our Lord Jesus will reveal Himself only to His own. For this reason, He said, "I will see you", and did not say, "You will see Me". He will be the One to reveal Himself to us, and this was exactly what took place at the Resurrection through Christ's apparitions through closed doors.

After the Resurrection, He appeared only to those who were with Him, sharing His sufferings: "Very truly I tell you, you will weep and mourn while the world rejoices. You will grieve, but your grief will turn to joy". According to the Gospel, the joy of seeing Jesus follows struggle, repentance and tears: "A woman giving birth to a child has pain because her time has come; but when her baby is born she forgets the anguish because of her joy that a child is born into the world" (John 16:20-23). Repentance to a soul is like labour pains to a woman: seeing Christ after repenting is like the joy the woman feels when she sees her baby.

Sending the Father's promise: Paternity of the Father

By now, it should be clear that the aim of the coming of Christ and His incarnation was to make us God's children and members of Christ's Body. It should be clear, also, that Christ is seated at the right hand of the Father. Thus, paternity is fulfilled to its ultimate capacity when the Father's Spirit comes to dwell within us: "the Spirit you received brought about your adoption to sonship. And by him we cry, 'Abba, Father'" (Romans 8:15). In chapters John 14 to 17, the word "Christ" is mentioned more than fifty times. It is the Father's promise: the extreme of the Father's giving to us. In other words, giving His Holy Spirit.

The Spirit of truth. The world cannot accept Him, because it neither sees Him nor knows Him (John 14:17).
"Those of the world do not accept nor do they know the Holy Spirit. If asked, the response would be: 'if they ask you about the Holy Spirit... say: God knows'. But we know the Holy Spirit because of our filiality, He is the Spirit of our Father. We know Him because He is promised to us by the Father. Christ sent him to remain within us" (John 14:17).

"If the world hates you, keep in mind that it hated me first" (John 15:18).
The alien world who hated Christ, Son of the Father, must hate us also because we are His brethren, the children of the Father, with the Father's Spirit dwelling within us. "If they persecuted me, they will persecute you also ... But this is to fulfil what is written in their Law: 'They hated me without reason'" (John 15:18).

"But when He, the Spirit of truth, comes, He will guide you into all the truth ...That is why I said the Spirit will receive from me what he will make known to you" (John 16:12-15).

This is our great share, through the Father's Spirit. "All that belongs to the Father is mine" (John 16:15). The Holy Spirit guides us, revealing future matters, firming our life in Christ.

He takes what is Christ's and gives it to us, bearing in mind that whatever is Christ's is also the Father's, and we are the Father's children and members of Christ's body.

The Holy Spirit: "And when He has come, He will convict the world of sin, and of righteousness, and of judgment" (John 16:8).
He will convict the world of sin because they did not believe in the One who came to carry their sins. He will convict the world of righteousness because Christ came to the world to call them to be steadfast in Him—to be seated at the right hand of the Father, giving them the Father's Promise. Yet they ignored all this, and He went to the Father without them, and He will convict the world of judgement because when God's children in Christ were seated at the Father's right hand, Satan was convicted. He had no share with God's children.

"You will be scattered, each to your own home. You will leave me all alone. Yet I am not alone, for my Father is with me" (John 16:32).
Even if the whole world is scattered, the Father's Spirit will never abandon us, nor will we be detached from Him. That is why, as Christians, we always say, "We are not alone. The Father is with us. We are on His right hand, and his Spirit dwells within us". Following Christ's ascension, the Church is no longer alone, nor is any Christian—regardless of life's ordeals, even if these end with death. As Christians, we are never alone. Instead, we are with the Father and the Spirit of the Father dwells within us. This has been the experience of the martyrs, the persecuted, the ostracised, and all who suffered through the world for the sake of Christ.

Oneness, Love and Glory

At the end of Christ's Farewell Prayer, He set three goals for the glorified Church in order to receive the gifts of the Spirit of the Father. First, He said: "... they may be one as we are one" (John 17:11).

He prayed not only for the Church to be one, but for the Church and the human soul to be one in the Father. When it comes to the glories of oneness, it suffices to quote the Lord Jesus: "I have given them the glory that you gave me, that they may be one as we are one" (John 17:22). "I in them and you in me—so that they may be brought to complete unity. Then the world will know that you sent Me and have loved them even as you have loved Me" (John 17:23). This is the glorified oneness attained by the Church, who is Christ's Body when seated at the right hand of the Father, thus receiving His great promise. The Holy Spirit is the Spirit of Oneness.

Second, Jesus said: "I have given them the glory that you gave me, that they may be one as we are one" (John 17:22). "Father, I want those you have given me to be with me where

I am, and to see my glory, the glory you have given me because you loved me before the creation of the world" (John 17:24). What glory could be greater than this? In Christ, we acquired a seat at the right hand of Majesty. Compared to the greatness our spirit received upon the ascension of the Lord Jesus, the whole world is counted as at a loss.

Finally, Jesus said: "I have made you known to them, and will continue to make you known in order that the love you have for me may be in them and that I myself may be in them" (John 17:26). This is not the type of love that is of the world—rather, it is "the love you have for me". This is a divine love offered to our souls. As Christians, is there a gift greater than this one we have received? The answer, of course, is no: what we have received was a pouring of the Father's love in us through the Holy Spirit. "God's love has been poured out into our hearts through the Holy Spirit" (Romans 5:5).

Let us open our hearts, let us yearn for His love, and let us have a share in this divine love that pours from the Father into the Son. This love is the share of the souls who are in the bosom of the Father, for ever and ever.

THE HOLY SPIRIT WHO PROCEEDS FROM THE FATHER

As Christians, we believe in the Holy Spirit who proceeds from the Father in the Son (on this point, see: The Creed of Faith for all Orthodox Churches). However, the Catholic and Protestant Churches believe that He proceeds from the Father and Son. In their view, this constitutes equality in essence to the Father and Son. Proponents of this view claim that the Orthodox Churches' stance constitutes inequality.

The Proceeding and the Sending

"When the Advocate comes, whom I will send to you from the Father—the Spirit of truth who goes out from the Father—he will testify about Me" (John 15:26). Our Lord Jesus sent us "the Spirit of truth who goes out from the Father". This does not diminish equality—rather, it reveals the nature of the Spirit. The Holy Spirit is the Spirit of the Father and the Son. However, the "going out from" or "proceeding from" means the "eternal ... the perpetual" proceeding, like the perpetuity of light emanating from the sun.

The Father is not limited. An unlimited Spirit emanates from the Father, settling within an unconfined Son. Therefore, if we say that the unconfined Spirit proceeds from the Father and Son, where is the final dwelling? Is it in the creation? The answer would be that the creation is limited within the human being, but what if we say: He proceeds from the Father into the Son? In that case, we mean the Divine Spirit, the unconfined settling in the Divine Word: The Unconfined.

God: Perfection of Existence

God does not need a creature to reveal His Divine qualities, because they are unlimited "self" qualities: perfection in His unconfined nature. (The "self" of God loves the unconfined Son). Here, we see the meaning of Christ the Lord's statement: "For the Father loves the Son, and shows him all things that himself does: and he will show him greater works than these, that you may marvel" (John 5:20).

His love is unlimited, perfect and eternal. It does not need a limited human being. Also, God spoke His Word without creating angels and humans to speak with them. This also applies in respect of all God's "self"—His unlimited qualities. Thus, we see that Christ the Lord gives (or sends) the Holy Spirit because it is His Spirit who proceeds from the Father. As for the share of the Father's Spirit given to us (the Believers): we are members of Christ's Body, and we are taking that of Christ.

The Spirit who proceeds from the Father into the Son is the share of the members of the Body of Christ—our share. "The Spirit of truth. The world cannot accept him, because it neither sees him nor knows him. But you know him, for he lives with you and will be in" (John 14:17). The world does not know Him and cannot accept Him; but we are members of Christ's Body. We know Him because He is Christ's Spirit, proceeding from the Father in the Son, and we are partaking constantly in our share, for as long as we are steadfast in our Church (that is, in the Body of Christ).

For this reason, our Lord told us many times to be steadfast in Him. Thus, we are to remain steadfast in Christ through our union in prayer, through our union with the Word of God, through our union via the Eucharist, and through the sufferings of our Lord and our fasting for Him. We practice this continually in order to reap the fruits of the Holy Spirit in our lives, leading the love of the Father to pour within us. This explains the words of the Lord, glory be to Him, when He said: "I have made you known to them, and will continue to make you known in order that the love you have for me may be in them and that I myself may be in them" (John 17:26).

The Divine Love that proceeds from the Father into the Son

is the same love that pours into our hearts from the Holy Spirit: "God's love has been poured out into our hearts through the Holy Spirit ..." (Romans 5:5), The Divine Love is a constant process in the life of saints, corresponding with their steadfastness in their communion with Christ. However, our knowledge of God is not an intellectual one, unlike scientific knowledge (i.e., reasoning and analysis). Instead, our knowledge of God is a knowledge consequent to our steadfastness in Christ, in whom God's Spirit of the Father is poured, and in us being members of His body.

Readers, I hope I have shown you how much has Christ given us as Christians: first, through His being incarnate in our body, followed by His ascension with this body to the right hand of God and, ultimately, by sending us the Holy Spirit who proceeds from the Father.

- He gave us His love: "the love you have for me may be in them".
- He gave us His knowledge: "have made you known to them, and will continue to make you know".
- He gave us His glory: "I have given them the glory that you gave me".
- He gave us to be one with Him: "that they may be one as we are one".

Therefore, as Christians, we should spend our lives diligently remaining in Christ. In this way, we receive the blessings of all these promises kept for us: "All that belongs to the Father is mine. That is why I said the Spirit will receive from me what he will make known to you" (John 16:15).

Section Two

Sunday Sermons

First Sunday
Thomas Sunday
(John 20:19-31)

The Lord Jesus is our Faith and our resurrection from the darkness of doubt.

The First Sunday (Thomas Sunday) of the Holy Pentecostal Period is classified as a Lordly Feast. The Coptic Church celebrates major and minor feasts. Minor feasts include: Circumcision, Entry of Christ into Egypt, Presentation at the Temple and Saint Thomas Sunday. Major feasts include: Annunciation, Nativity, Epiphany and Resurrection.

Thus, Saint Thomas Sunday is a Lordly Feast. Through the guidance of the Holy Spirit, the Church regarded the day of reform of the Disciples' faith as a Feast. This is because the Church recognises that any deviation in one's faith is a profoundly serious situation.

When we stumble in our faith, it is Christ Himself who comes and reforms our belief: "Then he said to Thomas, 'Put your finger here, and look at my hands. Put your hand into the wound in my side. Don't be faithless any longer. Believe!' You see, Thomas there are some who will believe without seeing ... Bless them".

As we consider the Resurrection in our lives, I want this point steadfast in our minds: Christ does not come to resurrect the dead from their graves, even though this took place during Christ's crucifixion, when He surrendered His spirit. Many of the dead left their graves at this time, entered the Holy City of Jerusalem, and walked therein.

Resurrection is an Experiential Act

I must be clear: It is true that Christ broke death and its power, and rose from the tomb. However, Christ did not come to resurrect the dead from graves as He will in the Last Day. God on His own is capable, without Christ's coming to the world, to set a day or a moment for the resurrection of the dead, when each person is to be judged according to their own deeds. I hope this whole issue is clear in our minds. Christ's Resurrection is an experiential act: it is part of the life of each one of us, even though the doors were closed.

On the evening of the Resurrection Day, Christ came while doors were closed. He said to His disciples, "Peace to you". The Disciples were overjoyed when they saw the Lord. When He had said these words, He breathed on them, and said to them, "Receive the Holy Spirit. If you forgive the sins of any, they are forgiven".

However, Thomas was not among the Disciples when Christ

appeared on the evening of the Resurrection Day, and so, Christ came again at dawn on Sunday. Here, it is worth noticing a gentle aspect: most of the apparitions of our Lord Jesus Christ took place on a Sunday. Although He could have come at any time, He came on Sunday. Accordingly, Sunday traditionally became the Day of the Lord. The Church assembles for the Breaking of Bread on Sunday. You may notice that some who converted to Christianity were Jews originally. There is a Church for the Christian Jews, some of whom continue keeping the Sabbath.

As you know, it is inherent in the Jewish faith to adhere to certain precepts, like the Apostolic Era. For example, when the issue of circumcision was raised and the Jews insisted that Christians be circumcised, a conflict arose as to whether new converts to Christianity should be circumcised. Similarly, the issue of the Sabbath was a matter raised by Jews joining the faith.

Jesus arose on Sunday. He appeared to the Disciples on Sunday and the Holy Spirit descended on Sunday. Thus, Sunday became the new Lord's Day.

The Resurrection: a Lived Life and a Personal Experience

For Christians, the Resurrection is much more than a story about people being resurrected from their graves on the Last Day. The Resurrection is a living practice: a personal experience in a Christian's life. The Gospel tells us that, after Jesus died, the Disciples hid together, fearing persecution from the Jews. Jesus came and stood among them, saying: "Peace to you". He showed the Disciples His hands, His feet, and His wounds.

Most of us have heard the phrase, "dying of fear"; the Disciples were dying of fear until Jesus arrived. This reminds us that death does not come from outside of us—it is within us. It is death because it is the absence of faith. The Disciples forgot Christ's promises and His words. This was obvious when He reprimanded the Disciples for arguing as they walked to Emmaus. Jesus was saying to them, "Why are you being slow and hesitant?" Thus, fear is one of the deadliest illnesses—it is death.

In order to resurrect the Disciples from their fear, Christ came into the Upper Room in which they were hiding. He said, "Peace to you", and in that instant, the Disciples' fear disappeared. Indeed, we're told that they were overjoyed. This total contrast, from sadness and fear to joy, is the Resurrection. How did this all happen though? As Christians, how are we to invite Jesus into our lives to cast away our fear?

The answer is that He enters through closed doors. This is the core of the experience of Resurrection. Although it's normal to think that the Lord enters our lives through open doors, this would not amount to a Resurrection.

As the Disciples waited in the Upper Room, they were in a state of despondency and despair. They felt certain that they had reached the end, that Jesus would not rise from the dead and that their faith in Him had been in vain. They felt certain that the Jews were looking for them and that, after finishing with Christ, the Jews would execute them. So they waited for death—until Jesus came into the Upper Room through the closed doors. Christianity never gives in to despair, nor failure.

Ask many people what they fear most, and they'll answer in one word: death. So, if death is the ultimate state of despair and failure, what does a person hope for in their dying breaths? They hope for respite from death. They hope for Resurrection. It's here, at this moment, that the Lord starts His work. For this reason, the Christian's heart is constantly filled with hope and resurrection—filled with Christ's reassurance: "I am the Resurrection".

Thomas was not present when Jesus appeared. Death was finding its way into his life. Picture Thomas' reaction to Christ's death: "there is no Lord. Christ was an illusion". Now, imagine meeting a so-called Christian with a similar attitude. "There is no such thing as God", they might say. "Christ is no longer with us. His story is hypothetical—nothing more than an allegory. Had He been still among us, we would not have suffered the afflictions, ordeals and pain that surround us". You might try to reassure this person, but to no avail: "No brother, our Lord is here for us. Of course, we experience suffering, there are crosses we must carry; but there is also Christ, who arose on the third day". Their response will be the same.

In his state of doubt, Thomas was dead but the Lord entered through closed doors, resurrected Thomas, and told him, "Don't be faithless any longer. Believe!" He told Thomas the prescription for faith: "the Cross was a stumbling block against faith, but if you reflect on it, if you reflect on My wounds, and if you reflect on the nails, you will believe". In this moment, Thomas felt a surge of energy through his veins—he felt the Resurrection. He said, "Lord, I believe". The Lord said to Thomas, "Of course you do: I gave you the Resurrection". The Lord told Thomas that Thomas believed because he saw, but that He would also give the Resurrection to those who believed without seeing.

The Resurrection is the act of our Lord, resurrected from among the dead. It is anti-death and emanates from within. The book of Revelation, in Chapter 20, tells us of two resurrections. The First Resurrection is the one Christ performs in our hearts and our lives. The second occurs when we arise from the grave. The First Resurrection is the work of Christianity—but how are we to identify other Christians? It's simple: a Christian will tell other people about the work of the Resurrection within them. Of course, other people may respond that the Resurrection of the dead is a long, time away, and will take place on a day known only to God.

The Book of Revelation Chapter 20 says blessed and holy is he who has a share in the First Resurrection.

Resurrection is removing the old being and wearing the new

The First Resurrection occurs when a Christian "puts off, concerning [their] former conduct, the old man which grows corrupt according to the deceitful lusts, and [is] renewed in the spirit of [their] mind". In its place, they "put on the new man", which was created according to God, in true righteousness and holiness. This is the Resurrection.

Naturally, if my existing body is removed, cast away and

replaced by another body, this amounts to the actual Resurrection. This is what will take place in the Resurrection, as the Apostle Paul confirmed: in Resurrection, we remove something and wear another thing. For this reason, in our belief, the Resurrection is about more than merely abstaining from sin. Instead, Resurrection is about wearing something else—removing a dead being and replacing it with one that is alive. This dead being is of the lust of the flesh—the lures of the world and its desires. We refer to it as the "old being".

This might sound harsh and unrealistic—we all recognise the pressures people face in this life—but, as Christians, do we believe that Jesus walks through closed doors? The answer is yes, of course we do. On this basis, we need not debate this point in more detail. If living according to the new being means that the doors in front of us are all closed, our faith tells us that God will walk into our life—and not the good life we strive to attain some day: our imperfect, very bad life, as it stands right at this moment.

If, as a Christian, you believe that Jesus walks through closed doors, then believe also that a new being will be created in your life, renewed in the image of its Creator. When it comes to our own ecclesiastical belief, this new being was created at the time of our burial in Baptism. For this reason, Saint Paul stressed that this being is renewable in our minds, according to the image of the Creator.

What is Renewal?

What does it mean to be renewed?

Renewal, like a newborn baby's face, is about changing each day. With a newborn baby, we keep watching for changes in its features, trying to work out which parent it resembles more closely. Friends keep asking the baby's parents: "Who does he look like?" "We can't tell", the parents say, "The features keep changing. One day he looks like his father; the next day, he looks like his mother". Then, a week later, the baby's features become clearer. As time goes by, with regular feeding, the infant grows, his features gradually becoming clearer. We call this a process of renewal—even though baby is an infant.

Beware those who go around spreading the mistaken belief that only when they reached their twenties could truly say they were saved. May the Lord protect the Church from these ideas, which Satan spreads around these days. These were never the Church's teachings. The Church teaches that the being was born in us through the Baptism. Of course, some people have been baptised but fail to manifest the new being in their life. This is because their new being is concealed and buried under their evil deeds.

Remember: if this renewed being is created when one is twenty or thirty years old, it would mean that one's belief in the Lord and their decision to lead a good life is an individual effort. That does not mean entry through closed doors. In that case, one would also be justified in saying, "I was saved", or "I was renewed" on such a day, or at such an hour—but one cannot say "Christ saved me". In my case, I cannot say that I was renewed on such a day, but I can say that Christ gave me birth in baptism. This occurred through the grace that was given to me, of which I was not worthy, and of which I was not aware.

In my case, daily I strip off the old man which piles up from the body and the world, as mentioned by the Apostle and by our Lord Jesus when he said, "Strive to enter through the narrow gate".

One may ask, "Today, and now, is it possible to experience the Resurrection?" The answer is yes—and if you wish to be clear about how this is possible, ask yourself: is the inner being within me in a state of growth? You may wonder as to how anyone can know that for sure. In fact, you are the only one who can know your inner state, and in the process, you will become aware of changes in your characteristics. You will begin to adopt our Lord's life in your inner attitude. It becomes renewable according to the image of the Creator.

No one saw the Creator. Even so, our Christianity depicts His image, His meekness, His gentleness, and His love. When you see your life beginning to be moulded into such a frame, you realise the growth in your inner being—the renewal in your inner being. This is why we call ourselves Christians: because of this new being, who is created within me and you, and who is renewable each day through the Resurrection. These characteristics permeate the image of Christ.

The Resurrection is a Daily Experience

We live the Resurrection daily throughout our lives. Perhaps, if the Resurrection must be preceded by death, it means removing the old man, and perhaps that was why Christ asked the wealthy young man to sell all that he owned, carry his cross daily, and follow Him. By "daily", Christ meant that we are to remove the old man daily, whereby it continues to be renewed each day. This process confers true peace through daily growth. This process is the Resurrection. For this reason, Saint John says, "Blessed and holy is he who has part in the first resurrection. Over such the second death has no power" Revelation 20:6.

If you are part of the first Resurrection, you are blessed and holy and the second death will have no power over you. For this reason, Saint John wrote in his Gospel, "but these are written that you may believe that Jesus is the Christ, the Son of God, and that believing you may have life in His name" (John 20:31).

The Meaning of Eternal Life

What does eternal life mean? It means life over which death has no power. There are two Resurrections. On this basis, in the Second Resurrection there are also two deaths. The first death is the one we undergo now on Earth. The second is death for an eternity of suffering. A Christian who was resurrected in the First Resurrection has overcome the first death of sin. This is the death that the Church mentions in the liturgy, "Let not there be death of sin for your servants nor let there be same for all your congregation". Whoever overcomes the first death will not be subjected to a second death. Instead, it will be a mere transfer.

Lies

"Therefore, putting away lying, 'Let each one of you speak

truth with his neighbour', for we are members of one another" (Ephesians 4:25). Lying is death. Listen to Saint Paul: be truthful because Christ is the Truth and the Resurrection.

Theft

"Let him who stole steal no longer, but rather let him labour, working with his hands what is good, that he may have something to give him who has need" (Ephesians 4:28). A thief does not stop stealing. This concept itself is not found within Christianity, because it is assumed that we should not steal. Instead, Saint Paul says to let the thief "... labour, working with his hands what is good, that he may have something to give him who has need". This is a Resurrection.

If a thief stops stealing, this cannot be called Resurrection. However, if the thief stops stealing, starts working to earn a living, and takes from his earnings to give others, then this person is practising the Resurrection. Remember: Resurrection is stripping off the old self to allow the new being to be born within you—a new being with an image of its Creator. This new being does not know theft but knows how to give. Once you remove theft, the new being is renewed within you automatically in the image of its Creator.

How does this happen? I don't know! I don't know how the Lord comes through closed doors. This is a subject I cannot explain, nor will I attempt to. Nevertheless, within my heart, I firmly believe that in my lifetime, our Lord will enter through closed doors. Nothing is difficult or impossible for a Christian, be it an issue, a sin, or any obstacle. For Christians, everything is possible: the Lord enters our life through closed doors.

Obscene language

"Let no corrupt word proceed out of your mouth, but what is good for necessary edification, that it may impart grace to the hearers" (Ephesians 4:29). This verse says it all: nothing corrupt should proceed from our mouths! You are a decent person and should remain so when you speak. What proceeds from your mouth should be words of grace—a blessing for your listeners that brings them closer to God. This is an act of Resurrection.

The Resurrection is an experience you live: removing the old and wearing the new, becoming an identical image of Christ in the process. For this reason, Saint Paul concludes by saying, "And be kind to one another, tender-hearted, forgiving one another, even as God in Christ forgave you" (Ephesians 4:32).

The Act of the First Resurrection

Jesus promised that once we believe in Him, we will be able to perform the same acts that He performed—and even greater acts as well. As a Christian, you might say, "Lord, how that can be? How can we perform greater acts than You? You raised the dead!" To this, Jesus responds: "Raising the dead is simple. You are impressed by the outwardly". Today, the resurrection of the dead is not significant. What is significant is the resurrection of the ugliness and foul stench of death that finds its way to our hearts.

Acts of the First Resurrection include helping a person on the verge of renouncing Christ regain their faith, or helping someone rid themselves of evil thoughts and replace them with a state of grace. Blessed and holy is he who has a share in the First Resurrection: death cannot hurt him.

Love is an Act of the Resurrection

The Epistle of Saint John is relevant to this topic, specifically: "a new commandment I give unto you". Saint John goes further, saying: "But he who hates his brother is in darkness and walks in darkness, and does not know where he is going, because the darkness has blinded his eyes" (1 John 2:11). What does it mean to be in darkness? It means being dead. In contrast, he who loves his brother is in the Light. In other words, love is the positive aspect of the Resurrection in our lives.

As Christians, we cannot celebrate the Feast of the Resurrection without feeling the act of Resurrection in our own lives, without feeling the life of Resurrection running through our veins, whereby we repeat with Christ: "I am truly resurrected". The Pentecostal Period follows the sweet days of the Paschal Week. This period is even sweeter than the Paschal Week, because we experience Christ resurrecting our lives on each day of the Pentecostal Period. However, for some reason, many Christians develop a feeling of apathy during this period.

Christ gave us a wonderful example. When He entered through the closed doors, He showed Thomas His hands and feet. He asked Thomas to touch the areas on His hands and feet that had been wounded by the nails of the Cross. After the Resurrection, when Thomas was asked, "Did you see Christ's wounds?" He said, "Yes". In the Book of Revelation, Saint John tells us that in the Second Coming, "Behold, He is coming with the clouds, and every eye will see Him, even those who pierced Him, and all tribes of the earth will wail on account of Him" (Revelation 1:7).

It's worth noting that, although a single person pierced Him, Saint John refers to "those" who pierced Him—plural. As Prophet Zachariah confirmed in his prophecy, "Then I will pour out a spirit of grace and prayer on the family of David and on the people of Jerusalem. They will look on me whom they have pierced and mourn for him as for an only son. They will grieve bitterly for ..." (Zechariah 12:10). The Book of Revelation also states that those who pierced Him were many. He was betrayed not only by Judas, nor by Peter who denied Him. Those who pierced Christ were many. Whoever commits acts against Christ pierces Him again. Resurrection is not manifested in their lives.

Nevertheless, Jesus Christ's wounds are healing. When Thomas touched the place of the nails in His hands and feet, the Spirit of the Resurrection surged through him. His life was restored, and he regained his faith. Thus, in the Agpeya prayer of the Sixth Hour, Christians in our Church pray: "O Lord, may all our pains be ended through Your life giving and healing sufferings. May our minds be saved from foolishness and worldly desires to the remembrance of Your heavenly laws".

It is not possible for everyone to enjoy the power of the Resurrection, nor can the First Resurrection take place in one's life unless they practise the joy of carrying the Cross, and experience the sufferings and the wounds of our Lord Jesus Christ. When, through the grace of Christ, we go to Heaven, we will see Christ. The first thing that will attract our attention is His wounds. Others will also see His wounds, and they will wail. They will say to the mountains, "Fall on us, we do not want to see Christ's wounds". In this moment, we will ask them: "What is it that upset you about Christ?" They will say, "His wounds" and in response we will say, "Really? These wounds healed us. Christ's nails nailed our weaknesses, our lust, and our evil intentions. These nails burst in us the spring of the Resurrection".

The Resurrection is Life

The First Resurrection is no longer a pastime conversation or a passing celebration. The Resurrection is a practised life, in the same manner that we practise carrying the Cross. The Resurrection has the same power. It is practised while the doors are closed. It is practised when we lose hope in everything. It is in those moments that we live and practise the Resurrection. Consider the Eucharist. It is the Resurrection whereby we receive the slain body of Christ and eat it. We live with the slain Christ, and the life-giving Christ gives us eternal life. As a result, the second death will have no power over us.

Consider also the living water of the Samaritan Woman. The Gospel about the Samaritan Woman is read during the Resurrection and the Great Lent. Why? Because the Holy Spirit works in our life through the power of the Resurrection. Why is water symbolic of the Holy Spirit? When Christ was pierced, blood and water came out of His side. Christ was not dead—an indication that the Church was to be born from the side of Christ. Water is symbolic of the Holy Spirit, who works within the Church.

The Resurrection has many definitions, which I shall explain later in this book.

In a reminder to remove the old and become renewed through our Baptism, the Church commences the Pentecostal Period with the Feast of Thomas Sunday. In the process, we are renewed in the image of our Creator. The Church teaches us that Resurrection is not merely refraining from sin—it also requires us to do well. As Saint Paul said: "Let him who stole steal no longer, but rather let him labour, working with his hands what is good, that he may have something to give him who has need" and "Let no corrupt word proceed out of your mouth, but what is good for necessary edification, that it may impart grace to the hearers".

We feel the Resurrection within our lives. We experience it and we proclaim, "Christ is risen", like the Disciples who hid in deadly fear until He entered through the closed doors. The moment He said, "Peace unto you", the Disciples' fear was replaced by Christ's joy. This is the Resurrection.

Thomas, by nature, was a doubtful person. He may have even doubted the existence of Christ. However, Christ entered through the closed doors and asked Thomas to feel where the nails of the Cross had pierced His skin. Resurrection surged into Thomas' heart, and he said: "Lord, I believe". The Pentecostal Period lasts for fifty days. Some say this is a long time, leading people to become apathetic, especially with the breaking of the fast and the laziness that develops consequent to consuming rich foods. These people argue that, during the Great Lent, the Church was in a spiritual high.

I argue that these people do not understand the concept of

the Resurrection. If they did, each day they would reflect: "Lord, we rise with you daily, we carry your cross daily". Fifty days is barely enough time for the daily renewal of our inner being, our minds and our thoughts. In order to acquire the image of Christ, renewal must take place daily—not just for fifty days.

In the Pentecostal Period, we should place our hope in Christ. We should pray for Him to fulfil for us in seconds that which takes hundreds of days:

Our Lord, Jesus Christ, may you enter our lives through all the closed door, because You are the True Light who removes the darkness from within. You are the true purity, who cleanses all impurities. You crush every evil, filling our lives with peace. You are the true Love, removing all hatred and replacing it with sincere love.

We must live the Resurrection because Christ said, "I am the Resurrection". He did not say, "I will resurrect you".

Blessed and holy is he who has a share in the First Resurrection. Death cannot hurt him.

Second Sunday
Jesus the Bread of Life
(John 6:35-45)

In this week of the Pentecostal Period, our Church draws readings from chapter Six of John's Gospel. Naturally, through the guidance of the Holy Spirit, the Church selected these readings as the theme of our reflection during the second week of the Holy Resurrection.

The whole subject of these readings is the Resurrection—which, as noted earlier, is not the resurrection of our bodies on the Last Day for which Christ had come. The Resurrection is our Lord seeing the fallen of humankind—deeply fallen and extremely weak. He came to save mankind. For this reason, in the Book of Revelation, our Preacher, the beloved John, says, "Blessed and holy is he who has part in the first resurrection. Over such the second death has no power" (Revelation 20:6). Christ came so that we may live our first Resurrection, over which the second death has no power.

The Resurrection is the Broken Body

The Second Resurrection will be easy: we shall fear death, because we triumphed over it in the person of Christ. As of today, this is our share in Jesus Christ, which we received in His Holy Resurrection. As mentioned by Saint John, He has resurrected us with Him. Partaking in the sacrament of receiving our Lord's body and blood is among the most important means of experiencing the Resurrection in our present time.

Hence, the Church dedicated the second Sunday (or the whole of the second week) of the Pentecostal Period to our participation in His body and blood. This is the first topic the Church discusses in the series of topics associated with the Holy Resurrection. This is because the broken body is also the life-giving body, so that people understand the Resurrection of Christ in literal, rather than hypothetical terms. In Church, the Resurrection lies before your eyes on the altar—a broken body, but alive. A lamb as if slain, for you to take and eat, take and drink.

The Eucharist: Experiencing the Power of the Resurrection

"Whoever eats My flesh and drinks My blood has eternal life" (John 6:54). We experience the Resurrection in the sacrament of the Eucharist. Hence, the liturgy: "Each time you eat of this bread, and drink from this cup, you preach my death and proclaim my Resurrection and remember me until I come". The partaking in the body and blood of the Lord is experiencing the power of the Resurrection and Christ's Second Coming, despite the indefinite progress of existence. In Christ, the definition of time does not exist: it is eternity.

Again, I refer to John 6. I know I sound repetitive but in order to absorb this chapter of Saint John's Gospel, we need to read it slowly and profoundly. In Christ's ministry, He fed crowds of 5,000 men. Naturally, this was a powerful miracle. If through simple words, or through a simple prayer before each meal, He could feed 5,000, then it follows that He can also give life. What life though? The crowds in His ministry ate—and then what?

The answer is that then, the crowds expect the same again. The Lord wanted to show the crowds the magnitude of His miracle. However, feeding 5,000 men—even the sheer quantity of food itself—was an event that could be forgotten in seconds. So often, we see the Lord's miracles with our own eyes: and then we forget them. When the Apostles faced the storm, screaming, "We will drown", He joined them in their ship. He reassured them, "Do not be afraid". Clearly, this miracle had no impact on the Apostles' inner beings.

What impact does a miracle have upon the life of a Christian? And where does one's miracle lie? The crowds He fed said, "Yes, we experienced a miracle". Immediately after, they started talking about the manna that fell from Heaven—to them, that miracle was more significant. The manna was significant because it was not a one-off occurrence. It was a meal every day, one day after another, for forty years. What happened after this miracle? The Israelites said they were dying, even though food was falling from Heaven. Eventually, they died. The manna was a foreshadow to Christ's meal. He says that He is offering the meal that leads to our existence and our eternity. This topic is covered in John chapter Six.

He began talking to them about His blood and His body, which was to be broken. The Gospel tells us of the irony in this. When the Lord performed this miracle, there were 5,000 witnesses (excluding women and children) but the manna was front and centre in the mind of each person there. When He spoke to them about the real food, our Lord's Body and Blood, he turned around and all were gone, except for the twelve. He asked them if they also wanted to leave, because they were free to do so, since he wanted to talk about the Truth. Their unwitting reply, because the Holy Spirit had not yet descended upon them, was: "Lord, to whom shall we go? You have the words of eternal life" (John 6:68).

Now, is the Resurrection a show, or is it a spiritual experience? Who is worthy of eating the body and drinking the blood of our Lord? Obviously, not the self-righteous, but the one who needs it, and who acknowledges his weakness before the Lord. He stands remorseful and dies with Christ. This is the person who is worthy of eating the live-giving body and gaining eternal life. His feeding of 5,000 men was a public miracle. What was the crowd doing? They were watching! What is more, they were having a good time as they watched. This highlights the difference between a show and a personal experience.

If one of those who attended the miracle was asked, "What were you here for?" Their reply may have been, "Just watching. It was good, we were happy". They were bystanders. For this reason, even if everyone reads about Christ, or watches sweet scenarios within the Church, or reads the Church's history, it is all in vain without experiencing or applying these stories and lessons in one's life.

The Resurrection: an Experience or a Show?

Christ arose from among the dead. It was extraordinary.

When the congregation watches Christ entering the Church in His body, they may think, "How awe-inspiring. He broke the seal of the tomb and arose". This is like the joy experienced by the Disciples: "Then the disciples were glad when they saw the Lord" (John 20:20). There is a difference between this situation and the situation experienced by Thomas. Thomas touched Christ's wounds, proclaiming: "My Lord and my God!" Even so, both Thomas and the Disciples were true witnesses to Christ's Resurrection. Hence, the impact of the Resurrection remained throughout their lives.

Is the Eucharist a personal experience, or is it the true miracle? The sacrament of the Eucharist is never a show. The miracle of Jesus feeding the 5,000 was a public miracle, while the sacrament of the Eucharist is a personal experience. In the feeding of the 5,000 men undertook the preparations required in order to put on a show: the seating of the 5,000, the distribution of the food, the surplus of the food, the collection of the leftovers, and so on. Christ came for the actual miracle. He came to give real life. He came to change us from within. This is the actual miracle.

His miracles were not confined to raising the dead or feeding the 5,000—miracles for the simple people. The actual miracle was when He gave us His life-giving Body and Blood. This is the intended concept of experiential Resurrection.

In general, people understand the concept of miracles to mean things they can see physically or hear about. People discuss miracles they have heard of all the time: "Did you hear about the miracle in Saint George's Church?" Or the Virgin's miracle in several locations. This is good, because God is glorified among His saints. He is the same God yesterday, today and forever. His miracles are manifested in the Church, even among non-Christians. We experience the most powerful miracle on the altar, whereby our feelings change and become reset in preparation for Resurrection with Christ. This is an inner miracle.

The Resurrection as Reality

After the feeding of the 5,000, the Disciples were placed in a difficult situation. Christ made the Disciples take a boat in the dark, and they found themselves in stormy weather in the middle of the sea. I leave it to you, reader, to imagine the fear and anxiety they must have felt. It was a similar situation to the dawn of the Resurrection. Then, in the middle of the storm, the Disciples saw Jesus walking on the water. He found the Disciples shaking with fear. This situation was similar to when the Disciples were in the Upper Room, with all the doors closed, and Jesus entered through the closed doors.

Jesus walked on the water: was that normal? Of course not— just like walking through closed doors is not normal. In a normal situation, in order to reach the Disciples in the storm Jesus would have had to catch another boat, but there was no other boat there: "On the following day, when the people who were standing on the other side of the sea saw that there was no other boat there" (John 6:22). The Disciples had taken the only boat available. They did not even foresee that Jesus could find another boat to join them.

A person who does not experience the Resurrection suffers from an absence of reassurance. This may lead to a state of despondency, anxiety, and failure. As you may be aware, in the twenty-first century, anxiety is a serious problem and appears in many forms. Some people even reach a stage of introversion whereby they end up shunning people and society.

Jesus reassures us not to fear those who would kill our bodies, since there will come a time when, "They will put you out of the synagogues; yes, the time is coming that whoever kills you will think that he offers God service" (John 16:2). When this happens, we shall be witnesses for His name, and when Jesus tells us not to fear, it means He has ways of protecting us. When Jesus tells the Copts in Egypt, "Do not be afraid", it means that He is in charge of their protection. If you were to reassure a person by saying, "Do not be afraid", it would mean that you intended to protect them entirely. You would not tell them, "Do not be afraid" and then leave them in difficulty.

It's easy to assume that fear reaches us from the outside. In fact, fear emanates from within our being. If this sounds hard to understand, consider situations in which two people face the same problem and one succumbs to fear, while the other is not affected. Why do you think Christ came to us? He came to dispel fear forever. He entered through closed doors. In what state did He find the Disciples? They were terrified—until He taught them that fear was death.

Christ is the Light. He is Faith, He is Courage. Imagine Christ dispelling the Disciples' fear. Imagine how they felt before Christ's resurrection:

- Peter felt extreme fear and denial; he was swearing and cursing.

- Thomas remained steadfast in his doubt.

- Mark took off his clothes and fled naked.

- The others, overcome by fear, each reacted in their own way, and ultimately decided to bolt the doors through which Christ entered.

The bolts were not the problem. The problem lay in the Disciples' inner fear, which Christ dispelled and replaced with the triumph of the Resurrection.

The Difference between Perplexity and Despair

Consider the scene of the Disciples on their boat as a synonym for the Resurrection. He entered the boat while it was dark, and the sea was tempestuous. These external factors affected the Apostles emotionally, but Jesus arrived to tell them: "I am the Resurrection". He arrived walking on the water. Through closed doors, even when the Apostles felt there was no hope of Him coming, nevertheless He came to dispel their fears.

You may argue that fear is part of human nature, so how can a person dispel it? However, fear is not part of our nature as human beings. The Apostle Paul gives us a beautiful description in his epistle to the Corinthians: "We are hard-pressed on every side, yet not crushed; we are perplexed, but not in despair; persecuted, but not forsaken; struck down, but not destroyed" (2 Corinthians 4:7-9). He tells us about perplexity and despair or failure.

Perplexity is a state of mind whereby one faces a problem and does not know how to approach it—but does perplexity mean that a person should despair? As Saint Paul states: we may be perplexed, like any other human being, but it does not mean that we should despair. In other words, Christ did not come to make us into a species that is somehow different from humans. He knows that each of us is exactly like everyone else on Earth. However, regardless of what stage of despair we find ourselves in, we ought to remember that the dawn of the Resurrection is near. Our Lord put it in three words: "I am He". Meaning, "I am the Resurrection; why are you afraid?"

The Disciples were terrified by a few guards outside Jesus' tomb. The sight of a maid led Peter to shake. Thomas was firm in his doubts. With their leader taken away, the Disciples hid, lest they be judged by the Jews. They were all under one impression: that their turn would take place after the Passover. They were certain that each of them was to be dragged and judged. Those who accompanied Jesus were known by name—each one of them. They were the followers of the revolutionist; they were to be triumphant through His death.

Fear comes from outside of us. The Apostle Paul says he experienced this many times. His second epistle to the Corinthians, chapter one, mentions that in Asia, the Disciples suffered beyond endurance, to the point of despair. They lost all hope in life. At this point, Paul was not desperate for our Lord's compassion—he was desperate for life. He disregarded thoughts of Jesus, the risen from among the dead. Instead, he immersed himself in feelings regarding his verdict of death.

Saint Paul demonstrates that he experienced despair when he relied on himself alone, and not on his hope in the Risen Lord. All he saw was his death sentence. Elaborating on Saint Paul's life further is beyond the scope of this book. In brief, Paul suffered imprisonment, he suffered at the hands of the Jews, he suffered a shipwreck, he was flogged three times, and endured multiple other sufferings.

Hope in Christianity

Therefore, it goes without saying that in Christianity, there is no such thing as despair. There is something called Resurrection, even though the sea may be stormy. However, let us assume that we are in the middle of a hopeless situation, feeling as though we are in a minuscule boat in the middle of a huge, tumultuous sea. Even in such a situation, a Christian has no cause for despair. Why not? Because Jesus came walking on the waves. He walked through the closed doors. You may say, "There is no boat around". I tell you, He walks through closed doors, and reassuringly He says: "I am He". The moment He says, "I am He, do not be afraid", you are already ashore.

The Apostle Paul experienced many troubles: "For we do not want you to be ignorant, brethren, of our trouble which came to us in Asia: that we were burdened beyond measure, above strength, so that we despaired even of life. Yes, we had the sentence of death in ourselves, that we should not trust in ourselves but in God who raises the dead, who delivered us from so great a death, and does deliver us; in whom we trust that He will still deliver us" (2 Corinthians 1:8-11).

Therefore, we should erase from our vocabularies the words "despair" and "failure".

Failure: Taking the First Step towards Resurrection

Paul reminds us again not to despair or fear failure in his epistle to the Romans: "we do not lose heart". He acknowledges the existence of failure; nevertheless, he also acknowledges that it is the first step towards Resurrection: "Therefore, since we have this ministry, as we have received mercy, we do not lose heart" (2 Corinthians 4:1). He emphasises this fact irrespective of all external adverse factors. Each day, our external being is subject to the process of extinction, but each day our inner being is also renewed.

Saint Paul teaches us that, in addition to despair, failure and depression that occur external to us, there is also an internal structure of hope. Externally, it is a process of extinction, but internally there is empowerment. This is evident in the lives of many people who endure ordeals and then find our Lord in their life, experiencing a surge of empowerment in the process. These people speak of feeling resurrected them from weakness.

Naturally, our external being follows the laws of the natural process of extinction. This is evident in physical factors that affect our bodies: ageing, fatigue, and declines in health.

However, our internal youth is renewed each day.

Constant Renewal

For this reason, our saintly forefathers never aged. On the contrary, as they grew old, their bodies shrank and their backs hunched, but they gained internal strength and vigour. Why? Because they experienced the Resurrection daily. As Saint Paul described so lucidly, "Therefore we do not lose heart. Even though our outward man is perishing, yet the inward man is being renewed day by day" (2 Corinthians 4:16). Nor did he stop at "is being renewed"—he continued to add "day by day".

In other words, Resurrection is no one-day, transient experience. As Paul says, Resurrection is a daily, ongoing process. Failure is present daily, Resurrection exists daily, confusion is present daily, and the absence of despair and Resurrection exist daily. Hence, our daily task as Christians is to remove the words "failure" and "despair" from our vocabularies and replace them with daily, renewable Resurrection. Tonight, when you go to your bedroom, pray to your Father privately: "Through Your Light, O Lord, we see the Light". Each time we stand before our Lord, we acquire strength from Him. As you confess and share in the Eucharist, your youth is renewed with each morsel and with each sip of blood.

The human being is like the lilies of the field. When the field dries up, the beauty of the lilies withers away, but the Word of the Lord remains forever. The Gospel tells us to focus on our inner being. Let us experience the Resurrection and inner renewal daily. Let us experience the feeling of being newly born in the Baptism. Let us renew and grow ourselves in knowledge and holiness, emulating the image of our Creator. If we use the word "failure" as the first step towards our Resurrection, then "despair" should have no place in our Christian vocabulary. Hope wipes out despair. We replace despair with a word from the Gospel: hope, about which Saint Paul preaches to us, "And now these three remain: faith, hope and love" (1 Corinthians 13:13).

In his epistle to the Galatians, our teacher says to be generous with charity and steadfast in Christ. If we do these things, we will harvest our good deeds in return.

There is a non-Christian proverb that is used in some circles: "Beware of the evil of those to whom you extend a charitable hand". What happens to people who extend a charitable hand? Some would have you believe that the recipients of charity will return goodness with evil. This is untrue. As Christians, we should continue doing good without fail. Christianity does not wane, nor does it despair. It knows a life whereby we wake up with Christ every day.

Saint Paul tells the Corinthians that we die every day. In his epistle to the Romans, Paul says that we die daily, meaning our Resurrection throughout the day. The Resurrection became Paul's life, as did experiencing death: experiencing ordeals, problems and closed doors. Experiencing the darkness of the sea, the tempestuous waves and, finally, experiencing Christ walking to reassure him, "I am the Resurrection".

The Resurrection: Success

This is the lesson presented by the Church in the Vespers Gospel. Resurrection is the absence of fear. It is the absence of despair and of failure.

The Resurrection is when Christ is alive within our beings, even if it reaches death—the death of sin. Our teacher Saint Paul tells us, "But if the Spirit of Him who raised Jesus from the dead dwells in you, He who raised Christ from the dead will also give life to your mortal bodies" (Romans 8:11). Even if we fail in our battle against sin during our lifetime, or become immersed in life's sins, rest assured that our faith in the Spirit of the Lord, who dwells within us, will also give life to our mortal bodies.

Saint Paul reiterates that He who raised Christ from among the dead is the very same one who will raise us, because we are members of the Body of Christ. I am a member of the Body of Christ, the Resurrected from among the dead—but how is this possible? Is it possible that Christ will die again? I am a member of His body: it is impossible that Christ will die again. The death Christ suffered was to happen once only, and His Resurrection was to happen once only. Christ will never be gripped by death again. We are members of His Resurrected Body. We will remain alive and the second death will never have power over us.

Remember: there is no failure and no despair, whether through financial problems or through our spiritual battles, but surely there is a Resurrection. Even if we reach death, God can raise us from among the dead.

Third Sunday (Vespers)
The Resurrection is Freedom
(John 8:12-20)

The Samaritan Woman was an average woman. Like many other people, she slipped in the path of sin.

Satan is neither gullible nor ignorant. He is calculating and scheming. He does not throw all his snares at once; instead, he moves one step at a time, dragging his victims to a bottomless abyss. However, the Samaritan Woman is not the topic of this chapter. Instead, our focus is one the well from which the Samaritan Woman went to draw water, and which Jesus stood next to. The Samaritan Woman was submerged in a well from which she had no escape. Why? She had married five men and the man with whom she lived was not her husband. I suspect that this was not how the Samaritan Woman had behaved earlier in her life. Satan had started her path to sin one step at a time, until she moved onto the road of no return. We do not stigmatise the Samaritan Woman as being of ill repute. On the contrary, we regard her as a saint for being able to emerge.

Peter also slipped one step at a time into sin. At one stage, "[Peter] said to Him, 'Even if all are made to stumble because of You, I will never be made to stumble'" (Matthew 26:33). Later on, as Peter walked around to see what was happening, he began conversing with the servants, involving himself in idle conversations even though Christ had told him to stay awake and remain in prayer. Peter went and talked idly with the maid—and then he stumbled! He saw the relative of the slave of the Head Priest, whose ear he had severed, who told Peter that he was one of them: "You were the one who did this". The maid agreed, saying Peter looked like them. Peter was in a dilemma. He denied, he swore, he cursed. He found himself in a lose-lose situation. How could he get himself out of this trouble?

Amidst it all, Jesus happened to be walking through. He turned to Peter and reminded him by looking at him with His gaze.

When we speak of Jesus, we speak of His gentleness, His sweetness. However, on this occasion, His appearance was piercing and authoritative. Eventually, Peter was released from the snare in which he'd found himself: "Our soul has escaped as a bird from the snare of the fowlers; the snare is broken, and we have escaped" (Psalm 124:7).

In the same way, when the Samaritan Woman fell into the well, it happened gradually, until she reached the stage of no return. Who could argue with this woman and the choices she had made? Who could solve the complexity of her problems?

At the outset, we need to understand that humans by nature are resentful, self-justifying, and arrogant.

The Samaritan Woman spoke with Jesus about issues beyond her realm of understanding. She told Him, "You worship in Jerusalem", positioning herself as some kind of professor of theology in order to conceal her real self. Then Jesus looked tenderly at her, reassuring her that He came for the wearisome and to help the heavily laden. He showed her that she was shackled and that He was there to break her shackles. He empowered her. This brings us to John Chapter 8, because this chapter speaks about freedom.

In Christianity, freedom is a concept totally distinct from freedom as it's depicted in the media. For Christians, freedom is not about politics—it is not the freedom of political detainees. Throughout history, Christians have been shackled physically: nevertheless, they remained free, because freedom is linked to happiness in Christianity. Remember, even someone living in a palace can feel enslaved from within. What did Christ say? He said that the person who commits sin is enslaved by sin, and if we are liberated by the Son, then we are truly free.

Resurrection is therefore a fitting theme for the Pentecostal Period: Resurrection means Freedom.

The resurrected being is a liberated being. When we experience freedom, it is resurrection with Christ. When we say in our Church, "Ekhristos Anesti" (Christ is Risen), we do not mean that Christ had risen a long time ago. We mean that Christ is risen within me—I am free. I feel this freedom because it is mixed with happiness, it fills my soul, and the person who controls oneself is better than one who controls a city.

Throughout John 8, our Lord speaks of Himself as the Light in a world of darkness. John began his Gospel, "And the light shines in the darkness, and the darkness did not comprehend it" (John 1:5). Christ's freedom enlightens the heart. Darkness is the opposite of light, and the worst darkness is that of the tomb, where not a beam of light can enter, and a putrid smell thickens the air. Hence, when someone like Lazarus emerged from the tomb after four days and the people said Lazarus had developed a bad odour, Christ answered that He was the Resurrection. They said that all Lazarus' limbs were tied, but Christ told them to untie him. He told them that once He told Lazarus to arise, he would arise: "I would offer him to the Church, and the Church would read the absolution and he would be absolved of all his ties".

Within the heart of the human being is either the Light of the Resurrection, or the darkness of the tomb. Saint John teaches us that whoever hates one's brother also walks in the darkness. This person will find themselves harbouring ill feelings and developing a multiplicity of illnesses. Ultimately, their behaviour alienates the people around them. Harbouring ill feelings is like living in the darkness of the tomb. When Christ steps in, then it is freedom, it is love, joy and peace.

In brief, Christ says that whoever commits sin is enslaved by it, and by all its ties—like the ties of the Samaritan Woman, which eventually crippled her. She thought water would quench her thirst, only to find she became thirstier the more she drank. When asked if she could do without the water, she answered, "Impossible", but Christ came to her just in time. He loosened and removed her ties and gave her quenching water. She began to recognise the Truth as she inhaled the fresh breeze of freedom in Jesus Christ.

Our Lord came to bless us with the inner freedom Christians enjoy throughout their lives. Among the privileges of this freedom is joy. This is our share in the Resurrection of Christ. We are invited to share in it, and our teacher Saint Paul urges us to remain steadfast in Christ's liberation. As Christians, we should not allow ourselves to be under the yoke of non-belief. Instead, let us be free always. What does this mean in practice though? It means we should not allow our hearts to be enslaved by anything or anyone, by any vice or any influence. Not by anger, grudges, oppression, lust, greed, vanity—the list goes on. Yet many of these factors are hallmarks of our time, and we see them around us often.

Augustine presents us with a good example that pertains to this point. One may tell you, "I own this, or that"—for example, a mansion, or a huge tower, or any number of other things. In fact, this person owns nothing: his possessions own him. Why? Because, while lying in his bed at night, he does not enjoy a deep and restful sleep. His mind keeps churning, on and on, planning, anticipating foreseen problems, speculating about the future. Obsessing over what he thinks he owns, but his possessions actually own him. Instead of being a master, he is a slave. He wears his yoke around his neck. His heart is under the complete servitude of his own desires.

By contrast, the free person, who desires to remain in the freedom given by Christ, utilises the world and at the same time loves his parents, his siblings, his wife, and his children. He is not enslaved by anything in the world. That is why the Gospel says, "My child, give me your heart". A free person is one whose heart is in the Palm of the Lord. Where your treasure lies, so does your heart.

When Jesus laid the precepts, He did not lay them for monks in monasteries or ascetics in the wilderness. The precepts were meant for the average Christian. So, as a Christian, live in the world but do not allow it to enslave you. The saints liken the world to a boat: a boat with no holes, sailing in the middle of the sea on which it floats. The boat keeps floating without interference from the sea. The sea does not own the boat; it only directs its path.

As Christians, let's participate in our share of the Resurrection and follow what the Gospel tells us. Let us be steadfast in the Freedom through which Christ liberated us. Let us not be perplexed by the yoke of servitude, let us not conform to this age, nor let us allow anything to control our minds. Let the only one to dwell in our hearts be the One who loves us and who died for us.

Christ paid a high price for our freedom. Our freedom cost Him crucifixion, death and Resurrection. He knows what it means to be tied, because they took him, tied him to a pillar and scourged him.

Satan is ruthless when he leads us to the path of sin. He lures his victims until he ties them to the slippery path. He is a liar: the father of liars. He presents his bait in the most enticing image, "If you come and kneel before me, I shall give you all the kingdoms of the world". Then he ties his victims and scourges them. Christ, King of Glory and sinless, stood next to the pillar and shared our humiliation. He was tied and scourged in our place. The sin that exposed Adam also exposed sinless Jesus. They crucified him naked.

You may draw as many concepts as you wish from the crucifixion, but bear in mind that regardless of your reflections, each suffering was meant for our freedom. His nakedness was the grace that covered us. We were in debt; He repaid the debt and nailed the promissory note on his cross. As a slave, I sold myself to Satan out of my own free will. Jesus was sold for thirty pieces of silver. Thirty pieces of silver is equivalent to 3.33 pounds. This was the average price of a slave at that time.

He was sold for the price of a slave to make me a master. For this reason, Saint Peter said that we ought not to undermine our sovereignty: we are masters. Whoever resells themselves to Satan undermines the sovereignty they were given by Christ. We became monarchs, children of the Monarch. We were anointed by the chrism of which even the monarchs, who at one time were anointed with oil, could not dream. We became the children of the Heavenly King.

Whoever undermines their own freedom becomes a slave—one who is not worthy to remain in the house, because they undermined their own sovereignty.

The Prodigal Son

This is among the most magnificent parables about freedom and slavery.

The Prodigal Son lived in his Father's House, where he enjoyed banquets and many other comforts. However, he felt that he was in a prison. Why? Because he felt his father gave him too little pocket money and was too strict and disciplinary. In other words, the Prodigal Son felt that he was a slave within his own home.

He thought he had no freedom, that the servants in his father's house enjoyed more freedom than he did. They left his father's house each night and returned the following morning after enjoying a late night. The son felt deprived of the simple joys of life. He was totally oblivious to his bountiful blessings. When he decided to leave his father's house, his father could have refused, forcing the son to stay. Instead, his father let the son go and taste the false freedom he desired.

So, the son left. Satan set him on the slippery path, where he was overtaken by the lure of false freedom for a short while. However, when all came to an end, the son woke up to himself: the false freedom was all a myth. He ended up tending to pigs and sharing their food—a stark difference to banquets he had enjoyed in his father's mansion.

When the son returned to his father's home, his father received him in his bosom with open arms. He slaughtered a fattened calf for them to enjoy together. The son enjoyed his first meal at his father's home. It was the same food he had once detested. What had changed? Now, the food had the taste of freedom. The restrictions he had resented were still there. The son realised that the restrictions were in place because of his father's love for him and desire to protect him. His father was like a mother who holds her baby's hand away from a burning fire, even as the baby screams, wanting to put its hand in the flames.

Satan is wicked. He depicts Christianity as a restrictive practice, between the teachings of the Gospel, the commandments, and its moral teachings. One restriction after the other. Satan paints his path as an easy one, its door wide open, but Satan's door leads into perdition, unlike Christ's narrow door, which leads to the eternal life—the life of freedom.

"... Anyone desires to come after Me, let him deny himself, and take up his cross daily, and follow Me". The cross is no longer the symbol of shame. It is the symbol of the love that was poured on it when Christ loved us to the end. He broke and crucified Himself; He poured Himself, as mentioned in the Bible. Freedom can never be outside the Cross: it is the passage. The wide door ends in perdition, and those who think otherwise live the same myth of the Prodigal Son. This is what John 8 is about: freedom.

Freedom: Returning to the Father's Bosom

Freedom is life in the house of our Lord. It is carrying Christ's yoke and applying His precepts: "My yoke is easy, and my burden is light" (Matthew 11:30). The freedom the Lord gives is neither false nor earthly. It fills our hearts with happiness without dominance, except for our true love for the One who loved us and died for us. He redeemed us with His own Blood.

Once freed, we are never subject to defeat. Christ reassures us, "I have overcome the world" (John 16:33).

This whole world, including its daily novelties, is like a theatre—but this entire world has been overcome by Christ. There is nothing new in it—bodily desires, visual desires, lavish living, earthly possessions. Since Adam's time, there is nothing new. Only new colours.

Christ was elevated much higher above our world. He was elevated on the cross and, from there, He drew people to Him, and these people carried their own crosses joyously. The details of the martyrs, who sang hymns joyously on their way to martyrdom, are beyond the scope of this book, suffice to say: "And those who are Christ's have crucified the flesh with its passions and desires" (Galatians 5:24). The Apostle further adds: "But God forbid that I should boast except in the cross of our Lord Jesus Christ, by whom the world has been crucified to me, and I to the world" (Galatians 6:14).

The Resurrection is Freedom

In conclusion, the Resurrection is joy. The Resurrection of the human being is his Freedom. It is the portion for all the souls who passed through the narrow door and carried the cross. If the Cross is the path to freedom, then freedom is the fruit of the Resurrection. As we enjoy our portion in Christ's Resurrection, we should remember that the Apostle exhorts us to "stand fast therefore in the liberty by which Christ has made us free, and do not be entangled again with a yoke of bondage" (Galatians 5:1).

May the Lord bless us with the graces of experiencing the depth of the Resurrection in our life.

Third Sunday
Jesus the Living Water
(John 4:1-42)

The Church sets the Samaritan Woman as the Gospel Reading for the Third Week of the Holy Pentecostal Period.

So far, we have discussed the concept of eternal life, or Resurrection, in Christ's person being placed on the Church altar: "who eats me, lives for ever". Now, let's consider Resurrection from another perspective.

In the case of Lazarus, who was tied and buried inside a tomb, it was simple for our Lord Jesus Christ to say, "Lazarus, come forth"—much easier than resurrecting a soul.

Resurrection of bodies is much easier than resurrection of a soul. We can deduce this point from the long dialogue between our Lord Jesus and the Samaritan Woman as He sought to resurrect her from the tomb in which she was confined (in contrast, the Resurrection of Lazarus is a very short dialogue). Jesus had to present Himself to the Samaritan

Woman as the one in need: "Please, give me water to drink". Then, things got more complicated—Jesus was a Jew, and she was a Samaritan. They were not the same. Old prejudices came to the surface. If a Jew passed a Samaritan in a street, they would not have greeted each other—and now Jesus was asking the Samaritan Woman for a drink?

Our Lord Jesus was not in need of the water from the Samaritan Woman, but He tried His best to resurrect this poor woman. He began by talking to her about the living water. He discussed religious issues with her. She argued that the Samaritans were in a better situation than the Jews. They were privileged, they had the well of Jacob, from which he and all his descendants and all his cattle drank, while the Jews boasted about Jerusalem.

Listening to this dialogue, and considering that Jesus once said we would perform greater works than He did, I wonder what greater works he was referring to. Is the greatness of work gauged by its nature—for example, if someone is resurrected from the dead? What if someone is transformed from a life of sin into a penitent life, becoming a servant of Christ, even an Evangelist? Is that kind of work greater and more challenging than resurrecting a person's physical body?

As I mentioned earlier, Lazarus was raised with one sentence: "Lazarus, come forth". However, resurrecting the Samaritan Woman took Christ a long time. Even His own disciples did not understand what was involved, and how much effort it took Him. Upon their return, they offered him food, but He told them that He had already eaten. They thought that someone might have brought Him food while they were away and laughed at Him among themselves, thinking of how He was talking to a woman.

They did not realise that the Lord Jesus Christ was not resurrecting a body from a tomb but a soul from the depths of hell.

Christ opens our eyes to reveal the mightiness of His act for our redemption through his crucifixion. We mention this in the Liturgy: "He descended from the cross to hell". Saint Peter mentioned that he went and evangelised to people in prisons and dungeons. The Prophet Zachariah says, "Return to the stronghold, you prisoners of hope" (Zechariah 9:12). In other words, come out of the dungeon to be liberated through the covenant of His Blood. Come out, you prisoners of hope.

I wish to emphasise that resurrecting the dead from their tombs is a simple matter compared to Christ's resurrection of the Samaritan Woman.

The Church follows this path. Consider the penitent Saint Paessa, whose house was a brothel. Saint Pesarion left his Monastery to draw Saint Paessa to penitence. It was a mammoth effort. He thought, "Instead of this woman luring thousands of young men, I will try to save her". He borrowed one pound and worked as a domestic servant in the house of that evil woman. He persevered until he took her to the convent. These were heroic acts, greater than raising the dead.

What is the relationship between the Samaritan Woman and the Resurrection of the Dead? What about the effort Christ had made to resurrect the Samaritan Woman? Isn't it the same as saving a drowning person? Let's say I am drowning: I need Christ to hold this dialogue with me. At the end of the dialogue, I need to undo all the harmful ties binding me—and the same applies to you. This is why the Church presents us with this dialogue. We need this First Resurrection.

We have been talking about the First Resurrection: the Spiritual Resurrection, for which Christ had come in order to raise us from sin. We are not talking about the Second Resurrection of the body. Our Lord Jesus Christ did not leave the Samaritan Woman until she was kneeling at His feet. "Kneeling" means total acceptance in her life. What about her past? It was wiped out in a second. Her meeting with Christ undid all her ties.

Was it easy for that woman to detach herself completely from her past? Five men to whom she was a spouse, with all the related places and relations—in other words, a whole lifestyle?

Consider this scenario. Suppose we try to help a woman of notorious ill repute, leading to her repenting and becoming one of the Church's saints. Would this not be a miracle? This is our Christianity. It does not spread by the power of a sword nor by the power of an arrow. It did not come to reign on cities or countries in order to extend its domain. It came to overpower evil and defeat hell. Christ, who was resurrected from among the dead, came with the authority of His Cross to rule over hearts and minds.

This is our Resurrection. This is our portion of the Resurrection.

The Samaritan Woman was in a miserable situation when Jesus met her. She was entangled, like Christ's description in John Chapter 8: a sinner, enslaved by her sins. She was a captive.

When Jesus came, He freed her of her bondage. He called her to lead a serious life, free of bondage. The Samaritan Woman is the best image of a person who enjoyed freedom in the person of Jesus Christ.

Without being over the top, we all know that when we are under the burden of sin, we are chained to it. According to the Bible, this is death.

One of the Catholic Epistles teaches us that we gained transfer from death because of our love to each other. In contrast, those who do not love each other remain in death. This concept may be treated casually by the average person but not so by the Church. Whoever does not love is not alive: a person who hates is a dead person.

Many may not be aware of this fact. They come to Church harbouring hatred and grudges. They confess and they receive the sacrament. They are unaware that they are participating in these sacraments while they are dead. The Church tells us that if our hearts are not kindled with the torch of love, we are in the darkness of Death: "We know that we have passed from death to life, because we love the brethren. He who does not love his brother abides in death" (1 John 3:14).

Here's a simple parallel: when a person's heart is in darkness, it becomes a tomb in need of Resurrection. "Awake, you who sleep, arise from the dead, And Christ will give you light" (Ephesians 5:14). There are so many who are dead. I experienced this death and perhaps you have too. When a person becomes entangled and chained within the darkness of grudges, hatred, envy and jealousy with no inner peace—

this is living in darkness.

You may argue that this darkness has become part of our contemporary way of life, part of dealing with the people around us—but Resurrection is not easy. Remember, Christ resurrected Lazarus with one sentence: "Come forth". This is easier than trying to bring peace between two parties pursuing a quarrel against each other, or trying to ask someone to forgive a grudge they have held for years. There are so many other similar examples in need of Christ's intervention.

Christ the True Light came to light the way in order to resurrect us. He came to strengthen us in the face of our human weaknesses, to control our eyes and guide them towards God's glory. "But if your eye is bad, your whole body will be full of darkness. If therefore the light that is in you is darkness, how great is that darkness!" (Matthew 6:23). Indeed, darkness is death from head to toe. The eye may sin thousands of times, oblivious to the fact that each time, it is death from head to toe.

Christ summed it up for us: "The lamp of the body is the eye. Therefore, when your eye is good, your whole body also is full of light. But when your eye is bad, your body also is full of darkness. Therefore, take heed that the light which is in you is not darkness. If then your whole body is full of light, having no part dark, the whole body will be full of light, as when the bright shining of a lamp gives you light" (Luke 11:34-36).

My Lord and My God I am living in darkness. I am today's Samaritan Woman. I am the one in need of your call; please come into my life. Come and reform me. Untie all of my ties.

The bondage of the world's lust cripples. It enslaves all its victims, regardless. How often do we hear comments like, "I can't believe what you're saying—are you talking about that dignified old man?" Or, "Impossible, she seemed such a decent girl", and so on and so forth.

The Bible describes lust: "For she has cast down many wounded, and all who were slain by her were strong" (Proverbs 7:26). Satan had calculated his method when he enticed Eve through the serpent: "So when the woman saw that the tree was good for food, that it was pleasant to the eyes, and a tree desirable to make one wise, she took of its fruit" (Genesis 3:6). Was that the only beautiful tree in the whole of Paradise? Was it the most beautiful tree? How did Eve know that it was good for food before even tasting it? How could Eve know all these details by merely looking at the tree? This is Satan's way of painting lust in the most enticing image, leading to our inescapable bondage. When the victim tries to free themselves at a later stage, they find it impossible to do so.

The Church realises the difficulty of this situation. Therefore, it prays that the Lord will release the bonded. All of Lazarus' body was in ties inside the tomb, but he was not the only one in ties. Many people outside the tomb were also tied from neck to toe. For this reason, the Church seeks Jesus: "You are the one who release the tied and who raises the fallen. You are the hope of the desperate. You are the help of the helpless". He is the help of the helpless. He is the Resurrection.

Thus, the Resurrected Christ is mighty—truly mighty. He is not weak. The simple people think of us as weak when they listen to our Christian teaching: "But whoever slaps you on your right cheek, turn the other to him also" (Matthew 5:39). They regard this as extreme weakness. Christ defeated death with His might, He resurrected the dead and He bestowed His might upon His Church. The Church does not spread through materialistic force, which is the power of the weak. It spreads through the power of the Resurrection, as reaffirmed by Apostle Paul: "that I may know Him and the power of His resurrection" (Philippians 3:10). The Resurrection is the power that sustains us throughout our life.

Freedom is the Fruit of the Resurrection

Freedom is our portion in the Resurrected Christ. In an Epistle to the Colossians, Apostle Paul emphasises: "Since, then, you have been raised with Christ, set your hearts on things above, where Christ is, seated at the right hand of God. Set your minds on things above, not on earthly things. For you died, and your life is now hidden with Christ in God. When Christ, who is your life, appears, then you also will appear with him in glory" (Colossians 3:1-4).

Let us be like the Samaritan Woman. You may say, "Lord, I do not know how to do this". "I will help you", says the Lord. "I was raised in order to resurrect you. Now you are a member of My body ... Your life is now hidden with Christ in God" (Colossians 3:3). Meaning that, like salt added to a dough, we are now part of the Body of Christ. By virtue of His nature, Christ is the Son of God, and we call His Father Our Father. Where is Our Father? Is He on Earth only? Is He in Heaven only? God is not limited: not to earth, not to Heaven—not even to the Heaven of Heavens. He wishes to tell us that, since we are resurrected from the dead, we should seek what is above, because our life is now hidden with Christ in God. The Samaritan Woman's past died. Christ is our life and we will appear in His glory. If we wish to go deeper, our real share is the Church. We are members of the Body of Christ, and Christ is risen from the dead.

Saint Paul immediately follows his statement by saying, "Therefore put to death your members which are on the earth: fornication, uncleanness, passion, evil desire, and covetousness, which is idolatry" (Colossians 3:5). These evils lead to God's anger against the disobedient.

If Christ liberates a soul, He resurrects it from death, He unties all its ties, and He shines upon it with His own light—but what if this soul repays all these blessings by returning to earthly vices? "A dog returns to his own vomit", like "a sow, having washed, to her wallowing in the mire" (2 Peter 2:22).

O Lord allow me a chance. I did come back. I did. So many times, I did.

We still have a chance. For as long as we are still alive, and for as long as we have the resurrected, eternal Christ, we still have a chance. Saint Paul says death will never overpower us again. We are invited to live the power and joy of the Resurrection. Our life is hidden in Christ. He raised the Samaritan Woman because she was detached. After the Resurrection, we all became members of the body of Christ. The Resurrection is our portion.

For this reason, when our Lord Jesus speaks about freedom, He describes it as His own area of specialisation, whereby everyone in this world views freedom through a different lens. They speak about freedom in the common worldly sense, but true freedom is that of the soul over which no one has authority—and nor can it be granted, except through Christ: "Therefore if the Son makes you free, you shall be free indeed" (John 8:36). No other person can give a second freedom.

The soul who lives for Christ, who is born through Baptism, and who is hidden in Christ—this soul is the one who is resurrected and is worthy of enjoying the Resurrection from among the dead. "Therefore, if the Son makes you free, you shall be free indeed". Never allow anyone to tell you otherwise. There is no way to happiness except through Christ.

The parable of the Prodigal Son tells us that the son was in his father's house when his friends drew for him a false picture of the joys and freedom of the outside world, making him believe that he was oppressed, that even his servants enjoyed life and freedom more than he did. The son believed them, so much so that he joined them—and, not so long after, he realised the delusion to which he had been drawn.

Any Christian, who is made to believe, through outside influence, that the precepts of the Gospel are restrictive or are depriving them of the joys of the world is under a false illusion. This is the slippery path of Satan, a repetition of the episode of the Prodigal Son.

Christ is the only one who gives freedom to the soul.

The Lord's children lived freedom at the highest level. Take the icon of Saint Demiana, a martyr who experienced the power of the Resurrection. Demiana and many martyrs like her were slain and killed by cruel means. Even so, they faced death with bravery—a bravery that even their own executioners lacked. History mentions many instances in which executioners stood fearful and shaking before the people who were to be executed. The officer in charge of the execution of Saint Peter, Seal of the Martyrs, had to offer a reward to whoever carried out the execution because other soldiers were afraid to approach Peter. Saint Peter had a halo around his face, in addition to the bravery he displayed before his executors.

In the case of Saint Demiana, a whole battalion prepared for the execution of one helpless girl. At first, they tried to dissuade her from martyrdom through various means; they told her the Emperor wished to see her, and offered many other enticements and lures. Demiana told them that she did not fear the Emperor, nor would she worship his idols. She had no fear of the King, nor his idols. This is Freedom: a fearless heart.

Saint Demiana was told that her father denounced his faith. She wrote him a letter telling him that she wished she had received the news of his death rather than news of his denouncing the Living God who redeemed him. Again, this is Freedom: a fearless heart.

In our modern day and age, even a millionaire who lives like an Emperor or King but is in a state of fear is subject to die of any of the many side effects of that fear: anxiety, or any of our modern day illnesses. The Resurrection removes this threat completely. It cleanses the tomb and transfers our hearts to become a dwelling for God. It fills them with the light of the Resurrection.

As Christians, we should not think that these lessons apply to others and not to us. There is no one among us who has not experienced hatred. We all have felt hatred, including me—but, at the time, it did not occur to me that I was on the verge of death.

Christ came to transfer us: to put an end to our desires and to give us freedom like the Samaritan Woman, who was freed from all her ugly past.

May our Good God give us the blessing of freedom of all the desires of this world, all its restrictions, its concerns, its anxieties, its hatred and all its evil to enable our hearts enjoy the full freedom in the light of Christ the Resurrection.

Fourth Sunday (Vespers)
The Eucharist is Life

(John 6:57-69)

He Who Eats this Bread Will Live Forever

This verse about the sacrament of the Eucharist is repeated throughout the Pentecostal Period, because the Eucharist is life: that is, as Resurrection from death, it is equivalent to Life.

Our saintly Fathers placed the Communion of the Body of our Lord Jesus in the same status of the Feast of the Resurrection. Following the ascension of Christ the Lord, glory be to Him, they began to treat Sunday as a commemoration of the Holy Resurrection, renaming it as the Day of the Lord.

This day was dedicated to the distribution of the Body of Christ. Some say that, during the early days after the resurrection and ascension to Heaven of our Lord Jesus Christ, during assembly for the breaking of the bread and Communion, Christ joined them giving them the sacrament.

The Church laid down a strong link between the sacrament of Communion and the Resurrection, to the extent that a person's knowledge and vision of God depend on their participation in the sacrament of Communion.

It is easy for a person to read the Gospel and then discuss, argue, analyse, deduce, reflect and comment on it. However, as the Gospel tells us of the two Disciples of Emmaus: "Then they drew near to the village where they were going, and He indicated that He would have gone farther. But they constrained Him, saying, 'Abide with us, for it is toward evening, and the day is far spent'. And He went in to stay with them. Now it came to pass, as He sat at the table with them, that He took bread, blessed and broke it, and gave it to them. Then their eyes were opened and they knew Him; and He vanished from their sight. And they said to one another, 'Did not our heart burn within us while He talked with us on the road, and while He opened the Scriptures to us?'" (Luke 24:28-32).

The Emmaus Disciples were slow in their sensing and Christ reproached them.

He was their guest and traditionally, is it not the practice that the host offers hospitality to their guest? The host should bring the bread, place it on the table, and offer it to their guests. In Jesus' case, He was the one who took the bread, blessed and broke it, and gave thanks. He fed the Emmaus Disciples. It was then that the Disciples' eyes were opened, they recognised Him—and then, He disappeared.

Then the Emmaus Disciples went to the other Disciples and

told them, "The Lord is truly risen". Then He appeared to Simon. The Emmaus Disciples recounted what had happened on the road and how they recognised Him at the moment of the breaking of the bread. They knew it was Christ when they drew the link between Him and the breaking of bread.

We must acknowledge that our knowledge of Christ is not intellectual: irrespective of how deep one's knowledge of the universe is, when it comes to God's mysteries, the human mind is incapable of comprehension. The human being can know as much as is revealed by God—that is, as far as He opens our minds to be receptive to His mysteries.

When both Emmaus Disciples returned to the Apostles, they summed it up: we recognised Him in the moment that He broke the bread for us. In that moment, their eyes were opened. That was when they saw the true, resurrected Christ. For this reason, our understanding of the Resurrection is linked intricately to our eating the bread the Body of the Lord and drinking the wine of His Blood. Saint Paul is guided by the divine revelation: "For as often as you eat this bread and drink this cup, you proclaim the Lord's death till He comes" (1 Corinthians 11:26)

Hence, our first step towards understanding our Lord depends on the enlightenment that occurs within our hearts and minds upon receiving His Body and Blood. This is not unusual: when we receive Holy Communion, we feel that we are in contact with our Lord. True, it is not a connection of an intellectual nature, but we feel the closeness, nonetheless. We feel that our eyes and our hearts are open while we are eating the Bread; we feel we are participants in His resurrection.

As I mentioned earlier, the Church linked the Eucharist to the Resurrection. Since the Resurrection was on Sunday, so is the celebration of the Eucharist. The Resurrection was at dawn, but now we conduct it later. It is supposed to end at dawn. The Liturgy of the Resurrection is supposed to commence after midnight, not to end at midnight as we practise it, because the apparition was seen at dawn on Sunday.

"Now on the first day of the week, when the disciples came together to break bread …" (Acts 20:7). This verse means that the breaking of the Bread took place on Sunday, the day of the Resurrection.

On the Eve of the Feast of the Resurrection, the Gospel of the Resurrection is read together with the Psalm that says, "This is the day the Lord has made" (Psalm 118:24). This means that it is the day of the Lord, on which we should rejoice. We say this Psalm after selecting the bread for the sacrament ("the Lamb"). Then, the Priest walks around the altar and the congregation responds, "This is the day the Lord has made". Since there are other Psalms for the other days this indicates that the Church understands that only the Resurrection Day (i.e., Sunday) "is the day the Lord has made". Those who attend Church early may notice that most Sunday dawn incense Gospel readings focus on Mary's visit to the tomb on Sunday.

There is a strong link between Sunday as the Resurrection Day and the day of receiving the Lord's Body and Blood. Sunday is also linked to the state in which the Disciples waited for the coming of the Lord through the closed doors of the Upper Room for the sake of Thomas. This occurred on the first day of the week: on Sunday. When He entered on Resurrection

Day, it was Sunday. Indeed, it's possible that most of the Apparitions of our Lord occurred on a Sunday. In the early days, Mass was held on Sunday only.

The Church views life as attached to Christ. "Abide in Me, and I in you. As the branch cannot bear fruit of itself, unless it abides in the vine, neither can you, unless you abide in Me" (John 15:4-6). How can we be steadfast in Christ? By eating His Body. It is the only way to stay attached to Christ. How can you tell if a branch of a tree is alive or dead? When you can see that it is firm: "As the branch cannot bear fruit of itself, unless it abides in the vine" (John 15:4).

Another thought comes to mind when we receive the sacrament of Communion. Death is the high price we pay for sin. The Priest in the final Eucharist verse proclaims, "And it is given for the forgiveness of sins". Therefore, whoever eats Christ's Body and drinks His Blood are forgiven their sins. Further, "forgiven one's sins" means their death is removed, which means the joy of the Resurrection.

A link exists between the Resurrection and forgiveness of sins. Otherwise, if the sin exists, Resurrection cannot exist and, in the presence of the Body and Blood of Christ, which are given for the forgiveness of sins, co-existence is impossible.

"Whoever eats my flesh and drinks my blood has eternal life, and I will raise them up at the last day" (John 6:54). Meaning, "Whoever eats my flesh" will never be overpowered by death. Also, when we die on the physical death, the Eucharist gives the Resurrection and entry to the Heavenly Kingdom, because He "will raise them up at the last day". He does not give us life here only, but also at the last day. The Communion is, therefore, our pathway to eternal life.

The link between the Eucharist and the Resurrection was established since the early Church. Those who converted to Christianity were baptised on the eve of the Resurrection. They were called the Catechumens. The concept was that the Baptism (being the burial) would be followed by the Resurrection. Thus, the participant would become worthy of eating the Bread of the Resurrection and the honour and joy of being paraded in the Resurrection Procession.

The Church Resurrection Procession is a reminder of the Eucharist. The participants sing the hymn, "Christ arose from among the dead. With his own death, He crushed death". We need to translate this into our daily life with Christ in practical terms. It is not a theatrical play, as described in some books (e.g. the Play of the Resurrection). Christ died because of our sins. He arose for our salvation. We do not attend Church to listen to sermons; we attend Church to admit our sins, for repentance, and for receiving the Eucharist.

We sing the hymn, "Christ arose from among the dead". This is the Preparation hymn before Communion. During the early Church, this was the hymn of the new converts before they attended the celebrations of the Resurrection. In the Pentecostal Period, it is the hymn of the repentant before they receive the Eucharist.

Picture the whole Church when all of us walk in the procession of the icon of the Resurrection. Not only does it involve the icon of the resurrected Christ: at the same time, within me, within you, and within the heart of each of us in the procession is the joyous cry, "Christ is risen from among the dead. With His own death He crushed death".

What does "With His own death He crushed death" mean in our own lives? It means that when we eat Christ's Body and drink His Blood, our sins are forgiven. Thus, death is crushed in our life. Therefore, the whole Church sings the Resurrection hymn in unison. This procession is the celebration of those who had Communion—like the procession of the baptised baby after Communion. It is a celebration of the whole Church.

From now on, you can draw your own conclusion that Christ arose once and left His Resurrection for the Church on the altar. When He said to Martha, "I am the Resurrection", it was the same as when He said, "I am the bread of life". The word "I", the singular first pronoun, is used in both sentences. He wanted to make this clear to Martha, but she could not grasp it at the time. She understood it later through the Church.

"I am the bread of life. Who eats Me lives the Resurrection". The Resurrection becomes within us. When asked about Christ's Resurrection, our response should be that each time we attend Church, we eat the Resurrection. This is the Christian concept we live. This is the difference between Christians and non-Christians: the first lives the Resurrection, while the second is an outsider. We are living because the Body that we eat is alive. We lead saintly lives not because we are saints, but because the Blood of Jesus Christ purifies us from all sins. Saint Paul reaffirms this: "Each time you eat this bread ..." The Lord told us that there would be a period when

He would leave us until He returns to us on the clouds. During this period and until His return, we eat this Bread, we proclaim His death throughout our life, and we die to the world.

"For as often as you eat this bread and drink this cup, you proclaim the Lord's death till He comes" (1 Corinthians 11:26). Further, in the Gospel Prayer, we say, "... you are our life, you are our salvation, you are our healing and you are our Resurrection".

Throughout the history of the Church, she has kept her faith as she received it from our Lord Jesus Christ. Saint Paul preached, but he did not add anything. He delivered what he received. "For I have received of the Lord that which also I delivered unto you, that the Lord Jesus the same night in which he was betrayed took bread: And when he had given thanks, he brake it, and said, Take, eat: this is my body, which is broken for you: this do in remembrance of me" (1 Corinthians 11:23-30).

Obviously, the Apostle Paul did not receive the sacrament of the Eucharist from the other Apostles—neither from Peter nor from James. He had "received of the Lord that which also I delivered unto you ..." In his epistle to the Corinthians, he allocated two chapters in which he spoke about the sacrament of the Eucharist, and how to prepare oneself to be worthy in order not to face subject judgment.

Without the sacrament of the Eucharist, the Church is lifeless. Why do we attend Church? We attend for Christ. We eat His Body and drink His Blood. This is the meal of God's children. When we are baptised, we say that we are "born from above". When we pray, we say, "Our Father who art in Heaven". When

He feeds us, He feeds us His own Body and Blood. This is what He has: life. "I have come that they may have life and have it to the full" (John 10:10).

After He explained Communion, most of the Disciples (and anyone who believed in Christ was called a Disciple) left. He explained Communion after feeding the 5,000. When He turned around, hardly any of the 5,000 remained—only the Twelve. When He asked them about those who left, the Twelve told him that not everyone was receptive to His hard teachings. He told them that that was the only way.

It's odd that, when Christ speaks to us about the life He offers us, our response is that it is hard, but this is the human attitude. We do not know where our good lies. The human mind is not receptive to the fact that God came down and became incarnate for the sake of our salvation—that for our sake He was born of a Virgin, for our sake the Great God died on the Cross and redeemed us with His blood—and, when finally He told them that He would give His Body for them to remain in Him, they left.

He looked at the Disciples and asked them if they also wanted to leave. They said: "Lord, to whom shall we go? You have the words of eternal life" (John 6:68).

Fourth Sunday
Jesus is the Light
(John 12:35-50)

In the fourth week of the Holy Pentecostal Period, the Gospel of the Liturgy focuses on the Light.

"Walk while you have the light, lest darkness overtake you; he who walks in darkness does not know where he is going. While you have the light, believe in the light, that you may become sons of light" (John 12:35-36).

If we follow the steps of the people according to the Old Testament, we find that after they had crossed the Red Sea, they needed a guide, lest they lose their way in a barren desert. The end met by those who lose their way in the desert is known. For this reason, God sent them the pillar of light to guide them on the way. The pillar of light symbolises Christ (glory be to Him). The desert symbolises the world. Walking in the world without Jesus and His precepts is identical to walking in the desert without the pillar of light.

We hear about people who lose their way in their car, keep turning left and right until they consume all their fuel and water, and end up losing all sense of direction.

The Church teaches us that the Resurrection we celebrate throughout the Pentecostal Period is a procession behind the resurrected Christ in the light. Saint John begins his Gospel "... And the light shines in the darkness, and the darkness did not comprehend it" (John 1:5). In other words, the world was lost in a wilderness (no less than the wilderness in which the Israelites were lost), heading towards death—but Jesus Christ is the Light. Whoever does not walk behind Christ ends up losing their life out of hunger and thirst in the wilderness.

Remember: whoever walks in darkness loses their sense of direction. This is your chance. You have the Light; walk in the Light so that you may become Children of the Light.

The Procession of the Resurrection

The Children of the Resurrection are Children of the Light. The Procession of the Resurrection is with Christ, who rose at dawn with the first rays of light that shone on the world. This is our way and our life—without Christ, we walk in darkness.

Without Christ's teaching, we cannot know which direction to follow. The Bible explains to us the nature of people who do not rise with Him: they live in darkness. Those who rise with Him live in the light of the Resurrection. It is similar to what is written in the Old Testament about creation. Earth was a mass of darkness, then God said, "Let there be light", and there was light. The whole of creation lived in light consequent to

God's word, for all generations. In the New Testament, we also have the Apostle Paul drawing from the verse of the Old Testament: "For it is the God who commanded light to shine out of darkness, who has shone in our hearts to give the light of the knowledge of the glory of God in the face of Jesus Christ" (2 Corinthians 4:6).

God, who sent the light in the Old Testament, also sent His Light in the New Testament: "to give the light of knowledge of the glory of God in the face of Jesus Christ" (1 Peter 2:9). I do not know how to depict this image: it is like a hidden light, which we do not see, and this light is concealed in a mirror; but when we look at the mirror, it dazzles our eyes all of a sudden.

The Light is not restricted to certain locations. When Christ came, He wanted us to follow Him in the procession of Light so that we may become the Children of Light. He says, "Walk in the light"—not, "I am the Light". He stops at that, restricting walking in the Light to the Pentecostal Period. The Church teaches us that the Resurrection is the real Procession of Light.

The Procession of Light (Walking in the Light)

Christ speaks about walking in the Light.

Only children of the Light walk in the Procession of Light, but who are the children of the Light? Is everyone capable of walking in the Procession of Light? Jesus said, "No". There are some who shun the Light, and Christ explained why this happens: "For everyone practicing evil hates the light and does not come to the light, lest his deeds should be exposed" (John 3:20). These people live like insects, surviving in the dark.

We do not believe that Christ is the Light of the world only, but that we also are Children of the Light. So, we are invited to walk in the Procession of Light: the Procession of the Resurrection.

Acts of the Light

Our Lord spoke of the acts of the children of the Light who practise the acts of the Light, so that "... your light so shine before men, that they may see your good works and glorify your Father in heaven" (Matthew 5:16). He also added, "Nor do they light a lamp and put it under a basket, but on a lampstand, and it gives light to all who are in the house" (Matthew 5:15). Thus, the Apostle tells us to rebuke the acts of darkness because of their nature (even mentioning them is shameful). "I cannot utter them": that is what Saint Paul says. Of course, acts of darkness are evil. They are not a Procession of Resurrection.

In the Old Testament, Ezekiel questioned why God was harsh towards the people. Our Lord told Ezekiel to come, and said that He would show him what the Priests of Israel had done. God made a hole through the wall and told Ezekiel to look through the hole, and he witnessed the evil within: a closed room, without windows or light, in which the Priests of Israel sat. He saw their sins and evil. God told him: "Do you see what the Priests of Israel do in the dark?" Ezekiel told God that, in front of the people, the Priests of Israel were good. God said, "But I make them accountable for their acts in the dark". For this reason, we say that our Lord's eyes pierce through the folds of darkness.

During their time of sinning, the Israelites said in the Book of Isaiah that God did not see them; they sinned thinking God could not see them. However, as righteous Joseph told the wife of Potiphar, "How could I commit such a great evil against God?" (Genesis 39:9).

The Children of the Light

The children of the Light walk in the Procession. They live the life and perform acts of the Light. They run away from acts of darkness—the acts of those who pretend they are clean on the outside, but are filled with darkness on the inside. Our Lord wants us to be pure in heart ("Blessed are the pure in heart") because in this way, we become blessed with the spiritual enlightenment through which we can see God. Acts of darkness do not befit the children of Light who walk in the Procession of the Resurrection. They cause not only darkness of the heart, but darkness of the whole body. Our Lord Jesus says that the bodies of the children of our Lord are nurtured by light, while those of the darkness are nurtured by darkness: "The lamp of the body is the eye. Therefore, when your eye is good, your whole body also is full of light. But when your eye is bad, your body also is full of darkness" (Luke 11:34).

Some bodies radiate light. For this reason, the Church follows the tradition of drawing halos around the heads of saints when painting their icons. You may notice this when you look at an iconostasis.

"The lamp of the body is the eye ... But when your eye is bad, your body also is full of darkness". I hope, as Christians, that my readers will take this statement seriously when it comes to attending the Procession of the Resurrection: when we attend the Procession, it is an invitation to the Procession of Light.

Saint John, the Beloved, draws our attention to another serious fact—there are acts called "The Acts of Light" that are acts of love. Those who do not perform acts of love are in darkness. This darkness blinds their eyes and they lose their direction. "We know that we have passed from death to life, because we love the brethren. He who does not love his brother abides in death" (1 John 3:14).

Is He not the Light who came to the world, uncomprehended by darkness? We are the Procession of the Light. We are the children of the Light. That is why the Apostle reiterates that those who do not love others also do not love God, because God is Love and God is Light. I urge you, reader, to keep this image in your mind. In the Procession of the Resurrection—the Procession of Light—there is no place for darkness, nor is there any place for acts of darkness.

Your body is light, your eye is the lamp of your body, and your whole life is Christ's Light. The Church describes the Cross as the lamp stand on which the lamp was lit, and the lamp was Christ Himself. He remained, giving light like a burning candle, until He surrendered His soul.

Up to this very moment, the teachings, the principles, the love, and the sacrifice of the crucifixion continue to give light to the whole world. If you talk about love, we have nothing but open arms: "For God so loved the world that He gave His only Son"

(John 3:16). If you talk about forgiveness, we portray it in its most noble image; none is more luminous than that of Christ on the Cross, saying, "Father, forgive them, for they do not know what they do" (Luke 23:34).

These are the acts of light that are to be practised by the children of the Light in order to walk in the Procession of the Resurrection. Through the guidance of the Holy Spirit, our Church picked up the concept of the Cross as the lampstand on which the lamp, who is Christ, was lit for the whole world.

Acts of Darkness

The Light is not restricted to acts only. It is also in our thoughts. When Jesus was asked what types of food Christians should eat, He replied, "Not what goes into the mouth defiles a man; but what comes out of the mouth, this defiles a man" (Matthew 15:11). When He said, "but what comes out of the mouth, this defiles a man", He was referring to thoughts. Indeed, when sinful thoughts are translated into words or deeds, these are acts of evil in its different forms: fornication, envy, and murder. These thoughts embody the utter darkness of the heart. I am not exaggerating: this darkness is darker than the real darkness. Perhaps one can walk in the darkness to some extent, with only a knock or a stumble here or there. However, when the darkness of sinful thoughts engulfs the human being, the person in question becomes immobile, unable to move left or right because their mind is in total darkness. The heart with no place for God's love lives in darkness. It is immersed in the perplexities of the concerns of the world. I'll go further still: people say that the world today is moving to an era of knowledge, of advanced comprehension—but these facts have nothing to do with knowledge at all.

There are many knowledgeable, educated people who believe firmly in witchcraft. They believe in the evil eye, in black magic, charms, and spells. They claim that, through witchcraft, they found written charms of which they had no knowledge, and nobody had told them about. Of course, they found these things: is it impossible for Satan to produce written charms of which people have had no knowledge, and which nobody spoke about? So long as these practices have existed, people have continued to find things that had been concealed. However, these are acts of darkness, and these are thoughts of darkness.

What about the thoughts of Light? These are the thoughts of Christ. They shine upon the heart. They are the light of trust in the love of our Lord, His Word, and His Teaching. The Bible tells us that He teaches the ignorant, and in the Psalm reaffirms this: "Your word is a lamp to my feet and a light to my path" (Psalm 119:105). This means that each footstep I take is guided by the word of His lamp.

My Lord Jesus, You are my Light!

Walk in the Light while you have the Light, because thoughts of darkness are evil: grudges, anger, hatred, moaning earthly losses. The world will come to an end with all its desires, and so will all the acts of darkness.

It often happens that a person is so evil that he harbours ill feelings against someone who does not even have him in mind in the first place. He keeps growing his ill feelings from the first stage, continuing losing sleep over his anger, darkness blinding his heart, obstructing the light—and all the while, the other person may not even be aware of his existence. Poor is the person who does not embrace the thought of Christ. For this reason, Saint Paul says, "But we have the mind of Christ" (1 Corinthians 2:16). Can you even imagine that the mind of Christ would have the slightest evil thought? Or think of hatred? Or worldly desires? Let alone satanic thoughts? Never: He says, "For the ruler of this world is coming, and he has nothing in Me" (John 14:30).

As Christians, we are children of the Light. Hence, we must exercise the acts of Light. In addition, we must rely on the Word of our Lord, because it is laid down to light our path and our hearts. What about those who ignore His Word? Well, they're free to do so. They choose to live in darkness even though it is clearly said, "Your word is a lamp to my feet and a light to my path". Those who do not walk according to the teachings of the Bible walk in darkness.

We all face dilemmas constantly. Is this decision right or wrong? What so-and-so has done. Was that right or wrong? On it goes. Rest assured that you will find all your answers in one book: our holy Bible. There, you will find the way to the Light is outlined as clear as the sun. You will find that the Bible cautions you against the way of darkness so that you do not stumble in it. However, if you ignore the word of our Lord you will lose your way.

We are children of the Light. We are called upon to walk in the Light. Christ is the Light of the World. He came to conclude our walk and to shine on the world. Christ delegated us to shoulder His responsibility: "As I was the Light of the World, now I give you this light so that you may become a light to the world. Be the light of the world".

The Procession of the Light or the Procession of the Resurrection is also the Procession of the Prayerful: those whose hearts are lit by God's Word, which shines on their path and guides them. Prayer is a pause before the source of light, reflecting the Light on our life. Here is an example: when Moses stood before our Lord on the mountain and then came down to the people, they told him that they could not look at him. He asked them why not: what had changed about him? And they told him that his face now shone like the sun.

Moses suggested that he could wear a veil; he put on one, two, three, and then seven layers. The people asked Moses not to speak to them, and for Aaron to speak to them instead, because they could not look at the light shining from Moses' face. It was not a physical light; it was light of divine Grace. It was the same when Moses and Elijah appeared with Christ on the Mount of Transfiguration. Jesus' appearance was of light, Moses and Elijah were in great glory. They were also deriving from the Light of Christ.

Be reassured and rejoice in the knowledge that, as Christians, all of our eternal life will be light. The Book of Revelations says, "There will be no sun" in Heaven because Christ is the Sun of Righteousness. He is the Light of our Eternity. Prayer is the nature of the Children of the Light, of those who walk in the Procession of the Light. For this reason, as Christians, we must walk in the Light, standing a long time before it and letting it shine upon us: "... with your light, Lord, we see the light" (Psalm 36:9). In other words, the light shines upon us, then it opens our hearts, eyes and minds. Then, we see the light, leading us to be children of the Light.

Therefore, being children of the Light, for us to walk in the Procession of the Resurrection, we must practise the acts of the Light and embrace the thought of the Light. These are of Jesus Christ, as it is in His living Word, and we stand before Him in the Light.

Fifth Sunday (Vespers)
If Anyone Loves Me
(John 14:21-25)

The sixth week of the Pentecostal Period is when Christians prepare for the ascension of our Lord Jesus to Heaven. Hence, in Church that week, we perform readings regarding the Ascension:

- "I go to prepare a place for you",

- "If I go and prepare a place for you, I will come again and receive you to Myself; that where I am, there you may be also", and

- "I am the Way".

We live through the Resurrection: The Lord's Resurrection, the Lord's entry through the shut doors, the Lord's Body and Blood and being steadfast in it, and the life of freedom within the Resurrection (an example being the Samaritan Woman).

Throughout the Pentecostal period, we experience different ways of learning about the concepts of the Resurrection—

its mysteries, its teachings, and how to actually experience the Resurrection so our life is hidden in Christ in God—until finally, the Church concludes by portraying the Resurrection in its shiniest image.

The Church shows us what took place during the Holy Great Lent, along with the Disciples' experience of the Resurrection (which took place before Christ's personal appearance to them). They were afflicted with fear, and Christ entered the Upper Room through closed doors, dispelling their fear and replacing it with joy. In their minds, the Resurrection became linked with Christ appearing.

At the conclusion of the Resurrection, Christ tells them: "I spoke to you about the weak aspect of the Resurrection. Even you Thomas; the Resurrection for you was real when I cast away your doubt because I appeared to you. But there will be those who will believe without seeing me and blessed are those who believe without seeing".

Christ speaks about Divine Love. What does Christ mean when He says, "He who loves me"? What is the Resurrection? The Resurrection as we know it tells us that Christ arose with a body of light. The closer we come to God, the more we live the Resurrection. In one of his epistles, Saint Paul says, "Now the body is not for sexual immorality but for the Lord, and the Lord for the body. And God both raised up the Lord and will also raise us up by His power" (1 Corinthians 6:13).

Saint Paul tells us that when Christ became incarnate, it was because He wanted to be attached to us, in order that we may belong to the Lord and the Lord may belong to us. He arose from the dead, and it will be this same power that will resurrect us from the dead. We may deduce from Saint Paul's words that the sublimity of the Resurrection is holding on to God, or what we call union with God. Obviously, this union differs from that of the Divine Union of the Holy Trinity. It was through God's great mercy that He came down, took a body and became human like us. The Word became Flesh and dwelt among us.

Hence, Christ began by asking His Father to allow us to experience the taste of the Resurrection: "that they all may be one, as You, Father, are in Me, and I in You; that they also may be one in Us, that the world may believe that You sent Me" (John 17:21). This is the most sublime experience of the Resurrection: "that they also may be one in us".

The word "one" may be read casually within this sentence, except for what follows: "that they also may be one in Us". This is a serious request. It means that this Oneness is unequalled, non-synonymous, and beyond human conceptualisation. It is a deep theological mystery beyond our comprehension. All we can understand is that Christ's aim in His Resurrection is to take us to this Oneness. His Oneness with us is a further proof that it is not our Oneness with Him, but His with us.

Let us set aside the fact that He ascended to Heaven with the body He took from me and you, and will be with that body forever and ever out of love for us. He wants to tell us that, when we become one in Him, we will be in a state of constant Resurrection: "always carrying about in the body the dying of the Lord Jesus, that the life of Jesus also may be manifested in our body". The Word always indicates that we live Jesus' death and Resurrection, always and without detachment from Him. Thus, to simplify the overall concept, if we are not in Oneness with God, we are dead.

What is a human being without our Lord? Nothing. No more than the handful of dust from which he was made. When Adam detached himself from our Lord, what became of him?

Had it not been for Adam, mankind would not have reached what we are today. Our Lord created Adam in His image; He breathed life into him. Adam was linked with God, obeying and adhering to God's precepts. Nevertheless, we were elevated to another stage. Christ came down, took our body and gave us His body, and we became in a real state of Oneness, a state given to us in grace beyond expression. Today, few Christians wish to listen to discussions about the Resurrection. This is a superficial approach to faith. The Resurrection, in its profound concept, is being steadfast in our Lord: "Remain in Me". For this reason, we in the Church speak elaborately about the Eucharist being steadfast in our Lord: that is, in the Resurrection. "Whoever eats Me, lives forever". The words "Oneness" or "One" are repeated often: "... that they also may be one in Us" and, "... that the world may believe that You sent Me".

Father, as You sent Me into the world, I also have sent them into the world.

Remember: Oneness in God is the essence of the Resurrection. At the end of the holy forty days, many people question what they have received from Christ—what has been the outcome? Of course, it is being steadfast in God. Being steadfast in God is life; it is the Resurrection. Detachment from God is sin. If you need to define sin, remember this: it is "detachment from our Lord".

See how far our forefathers went in improvising different prayers to bring them closer to the Lord—for example, Jesus' Prayer ("My Lord Jesus have mercy on me"), in addition to constant hymns. Our Lord's name was on their tongues and in their thoughts constantly. They were attached to the Lord at all times: during their sleep, during their coming and going—always. What does that mean? They were in a state of perpetual resurrection. This state requires purification, whereby the person is released of all worldly bonds and becomes in a state of attachment to God even while he is in the middle of the world. It requires spiritual maturity for a person to feel that their life is in God, and that there is no life without our Lord.

So, the Resurrection is the appearance of our Lord to the Disciples when they were assembled. Otherwise, how did they know that He was resurrected? They were sitting in their room, behind closed doors. They raised their eyes to see Christ entering through the closed doors. He arose from the dead! This is the Resurrection.

Listen to what the Vespers Gospel tells us: "He who has My commandments and keeps them, it is he who loves Me. And he who loves Me will be loved by My Father, and I will love him and manifest Myself to him" (John 14:21). Often, we make the mistake of saying that we will stand before our Lord. No: we stand and our Lord manifests Himself to us. Bear in mind that the Resurrection was a series of appearances.

The Disciples did not look around for our Lord, or say, "where is He today?" or, "Where did He appear?"

The Disciples of Emmaus were walking and, on their way, they turned and saw a third person with them. Jesus saw that they were concerned, thinking of Him all the time. He appeared to them—and this is Resurrection. The Disciples were thinking of Him inside the Upper Room, behind doors—and He appeared to them. He appeared to the Disciples whom He loved, whose hearts were full of love for Him, when He and Peter were fishing.

Thus, the Resurrection in our Christian understanding is God's appearance to the Disciples. We too are Disciples. How does God appear to us? Here is the key: "... he who loves Me will be loved by My Father, and I will love him and manifest Myself to him". Christ manifests Himself to us, not to the world. In other words, Christianity is not a mere ideology or philosophy or intellectual conviction. It is God's self-manifestation to humankind. One may question why He would manifest to us and not to the world, and Jesus answered this clearly: "If anyone loves Me, he will keep My word; and My Father will love him, and We will come to him and make Our home" (John 14:23).

Christianity goes beyond manifestation: it is the Father, the Son and the Holy Spirit, who come and make their home a permanent residence within our hearts. Here, the Resurrection takes the profound theological concept which the Church wants us to reach eventually. So, our discussion is not hypothetical.

Jesus is yesterday, today, and forever. His manifestation to the Disciples is the same, and up to this day, He remains the same. "Blessed are the pure in heart, for they shall see God" (Matthew 5:8). He speaks of the Resurrection as Oneness in our Lord. We may wonder, "And where is He? Why can't we see Him? Is the Resurrection the same as it was in the past?" He appeared through closed doors, and He enters our hearts: he who loves Me will be loved by My Father, and I will love him and manifest Myself to him.

God appears anywhere and everywhere: on our return from work, in Church, in our bedroom while we pray. How does He appear to us on our return from work? The answer: if we think of Him on the way, like the Disciples as they walked to Emmaus. He appears during our workday, like He appeared to the Disciples while they were fishing because they loved Christ. He appears to us when we gather in the name of Christ, the same way that He appeared to them in the Upper Room. The Resurrection means God's appearance before us. He comes, makes His home and His permanent residence within us. All that He asks of us is to love Him, whereby He manifests Himself to us. He asked this in His farewell prayer: "Then the world will know that You sent Me and have loved them even as You have loved Me".

This verse shows clearly the depth of our Father's love for us. It is not a mediocre love—it is equal to His Father's love for Him. He emptied the spirit of love within us, which is the spirit of the Father within us. These theoretical concepts should, by now, be embodied by Christianity in our minds. For example, when Christ wants to give us Himself, He says, "Come and eat..." He wants to feed us Love, to feed us Himself. The Holy Spirit is the Spirit of Love. He wants to feed us meekness; He wants to feed us Himself. Hence, the Holy Spirit is the spirit of love and, since He speaks of Love, He wishes to pour into our hearts a certain type of love, unmatched in the whole world, incomparable to mere human emotions.

In his epistle to the Romans, Saint Paul says, "knowing that tribulation produces perseverance; and perseverance, character; and character, hope" (Romans 5:3). Hope does not fail because God's love is poured in our hearts by the Holy Spirit. Therefore, when He says, "I loved them even as You loved Me", He confirms that He loved his own; He loved those in the world to the end.

Some time ago, I read an article stating that, when Christ broke His body, and when He offered it, He offered the Resurrection at the same time, because He was alive. The live-giving Christ was breaking Himself. You may also consider this from the point of view of the Crucifixion. He offered Himself and died on the Cross, but He was resurrected. For this reason, our Church focuses on Resurrection as power for the Cross. Without the Resurrection, the Cross would have meant that Christ died merely for our sake. Jesus offered the Resurrection because He gave His broken Body and shed Blood, while He was breaking Himself, because He loved His own. This was the ultimate love: He stood and began offering Himself while broken. The Book of Revelation says, "And I looked, and behold, in the midst of the throne and of the four living creatures, and in the midst of the elders, stood a Lamb as though it had been slain" (Revelations 5: 6-7)—meaning slain but not dead, slain but standing.

Therefore, the love with which our Lord blessed us is not comparable to mere romantic or sentimental emotions we exchange among each other. It is love through the Holy Spirit, poured into our hearts, the ultimate of which is breaking Himself to embrace us: "I loved them as You loved Me".

What does "as You loved Me" mean? Does that place us in an equal status with our Lord? No, because the spirit of love given to us is poured into our hearts through the Holy Spirit. This is the love we receive, not the worldly love people describe. It is not like a father's love of his son, a mother's love of her daughter, brothers' love of each other or a husband's love of his wife. He offers the same love His Father gave Him—meaning the Holy Spirit. He made us know His Name and continue to make us know His Name, so that we may have the same love His Father gave Him. Thus, He dwells within us. The Oneness He speaks about is the actual characteristic of the resurrection, as presented to us by the Church through the pouring of God's love in our hearts.

The Holy Spirit is the Spirit of Love. Christ ascended to Heaven and sent us the Holy Spirit of love and poured into our hearts the springs of Christ's divine love. For those who open their hearts and respond to the act of the Holy Spirit, He "will love him and manifest Myself to him". This is the Resurrection again: "If anyone loves Me, he will keep My word; and My Father will love him, and We will come to him and make Our home". Or, "Those who do not keep my word do not love Me".

Within this concept, the Resurrection is the fruit of the divine love and our Lord's appearance to us. However, when we speak about the pouring of our Lord's love in our life, our hearts must be receptive to this love. What is the proof of our love? "If anyone loves Me, he will keep My word". Seeing our Lord or witnessing the Resurrection means keeping His Word. That is the core truth from beginning to end.

God is willing to pour His love into our hearts and manifest Himself to us, enabling us to enjoy the Resurrection, making his permanent home within us. With His Father's same love for Him, He makes us one with Him if we keep his word. He kept reiterating this: once, twice, and thrice. Therefore, the essence of the Resurrection is keeping Christ's Word.

From this point, we begin to yearn, earnestly and sincerely, to keep Christ's word at any cost, because Christ will appear to us if we do. We will be one in Him, He will make His home within us, He will pour His love within us and we shall live the Resurrection in the deepest theological sense, which the Saints sought.

It is not surprising that someone like Saint Anthony, in order to keep the Word, went and sold all he had. With great courage, he placed the world under his feet. This man loved Christ. Was he worthy? Yes. Worthy of immediate appearance. "If anyone loves Me, he will keep My Word and I will manifest Myself to him". Surely, our Lord manifested Himself to Anthony and walked with him the way to the end, one step at a time.

Let us reverse this verse: "If anyone does not love Me, he will not keep My Word". What about those of us who are weak on Earth? How often do we break our Lord's Word? Our ego, our personal greed, ulterior motives, love of our possessions, bias, and other adverse emotions—all are in transgression of Christ's word.

Christ's word is precious: it is the actual Resurrection, because it is God's self-manifesting in you. It is the making of His home within you; it is pouring His love into your heart, making you one in Him as He is One in the Father. This is the concept of the Resurrection.

"If anyone does not keep My Word, he will not be able to see Me, will not enjoy My love, and will not rejoice in the Resurrection".

What would be the benefit of Christ's crucifixion, and His burial, and the suffering of the Disciples without the joy of the Resurrection? None. The ultimate joy was after the Resurrection, when Christ revealed Himself to them. What is the point of our Christianity if we carry the Cross, walk behind Christ, suffer on Earth, sometimes being humiliated as Christians, only to observe some precepts and break others? In this instance, we do not enjoy the joy and power of the Resurrection. So what is the point? It would be like standing midway up a flight of stairs with no prospect of finishing the climb. For the souls who are attached to Him, who love Him, and who keep His word, the Resurrection is easy, and the Lord's appearance is simple.

Christ's word is precious—but how precious is it to you, reader? Will you keep it with all your strength and courage? Because its fruits are great. You may be tempted to say, "I am willing to carry out all the precepts—except for this one". You are free to do this, but your loss will be great. You will lose the joy, the power, the greatness and the glory of the Resurrection.

Put everything under your feet and keep Christ's word. He will reveal Himself to you, pour His love into your heart, and you will become one in Him. Christ will be your portion.

Fifth Sunday
Jesus is Our Way
(John 14: 1-11)

In the sixth week of the Holy Pentecostal period, the Church celebrates the ascension of our Lord to Heaven. The church sermons used in this period reflect deeper meanings around the Resurrection, culminating in the Ascension of our Lord Jesus.

"I am going to the Father". This chapter, in its simplistic superficial meaning, sounds like it describes someone going for a walk—as though the Father lives somewhere and the Son lives somewhere else. Phillip immediately asked to know the route, or the map to it, in order to go to the Father, whom he knew the Lord loved and whom he had heard so much about.

Of course, we know Phillip was naive when he said, "I am going to the Father". Jesus said to him, "Have I been with you so long, and yet you have not known Me, Philip? He who has seen Me has seen the Father; so how can you say, 'Show us the Father'? Do you not believe that I am in the Father, and the Father in Me?" (John 14:9).

Here's a question: when you hear about the Ascension, do you envisage a path that could be described or defined easily? Obviously not: the Ascension it is the clear and perfect revelation that confirms the truth of the Resurrection. In Hebrews, Saint Paul says, "Therefore, brethren, having boldness to enter the Holiest by the blood of Jesus, by a new and living way which He consecrated for us, through the veil, that is, His flesh" (Hebrews 10:19).

Therefore, we are confident to enter the Holiest through the Blood of Jesus, in the new way He consecrated for us with the veil, which is His flesh. Our Lord Jesus Christ consecrated for us the way with His Body through His entrance to the Holiest.

How is that possible? Because Christ's Body, the Resurrected from among the dead, is the Church, and we are members of His body. The Apostle explained it: "For we are members of His body, of His flesh and of His bones" (Ephesians 5:30). When Christ, the King of Glory, consecrated a way for us with His body (which is the veil), He carried us within His own Body. He reassured us that He was going to consecrate away with His own Body. For this reason, the Church, guided by the Holy Spirit, views the Epistle of Saint Paul as revealing to us the meaning of the Way our Lord Jesus Christ discussed. He consecrated a new Way for us. Christ's body, the Risen from among the dead, is the body of the Church: "You have brought my first fruit up to heaven".

How was that Way consecrated? Christ, King of Glory, took the Church's body and entered the Holiest. From there on, He showed us the Way. The Way is not a physical walk or a track to be drawn for us. The Way is when Christ Himself carried us within Himself; He consecrated the way through sprinkling His own Blood and entering the Holiest: "Let us draw near to God with a sincere heart and with the full assurance that faith brings, having our hearts sprinkled to cleanse us from a guilty conscience and having our bodies washed with pure water" (Hebrews 10:22).

Hence, our bodies were washed with Baptism ("washed with pure water"), resurrected with Christ from among the dead. The blessing of Christ's Resurrection from the dead was not fulfilled until He arrived with the Body he took from us. For this reason, it became known to us from the moment we joined the Church (that is, the day we were baptised—the day we were raised from among the dead and "buried with Him in Baptism") that we too would walk through a new life.

Since the day we came out of the baptismal font, we were saying that we were born from heaven in the person of Christ: saying, "Our Father who art in Heaven". Christ came down from Heaven specifically to raise the fallen humanity, who had a veil between them and God. He raised us to the grace of sonship, ("this is the Way").

How can a person call our Lord "Our Father"? The first prerequisite is for them to be buried in Baptism, have a new Resurrection, and be attached to the Body of Christ, who is God's Son by nature. We are God's children by adoption. Our life, being hidden in Him, is the only means to make us God's children. Therefore, the Feast of the Ascension is the Feast of Paternity and Sonship. The Feast of the Beginning, whereby the first fruit arrived in Heaven, when Christ arrived in the Body of the Church, at the Way consecrated by His own body. The One whose blood paid the price on the Cross was the one who waived the enmity and the One who entered the Holiest, carrying us within Him.

For this reason, in this Feast (in which we started the Way) we also receive our Baptism. Thus, the Apostle was clear when he spoke about the Way, describing our bodies as being washed with pure water. The Book of Acts explains the repentance of Saul, who persecuted the Church: "... from whom I also received letters to the brethren, and went to Damascus to bring in chains even those who were there to Jerusalem to be punished" (Acts 22:5).

It followed that Christians were called "followers of the Way" and, upon seeing a Christian, other people would ask them: "Are you a follower of the Way?". Was this mistaken for one of the ways of worship? No, because Christ confirmed that he is the Way. Thus, His Disciples and His followers adopted this motto throughout their lives: "we are the followers of the Way". Christ became their Way and they, in turn, became the Way.

Jesus stopped Saul on his way to Damascus in order to guide him to the way. "'Saul, Saul, why are you persecuting Me?' And he said, 'Who are You, Lord?' Then the Lord said, 'I am Jesus, whom you are persecuting. It is hard for you to kick against the goads'" (Acts 9:4-5). Saul did not realise he had persecuted the "Followers of the Way". Nor did he realise that persecutions directed at Christians were directed at Jesus personally because they were members of Jesus' Body, because He had them within His own body. When he stoned Stephen, each stone was directed at Him.

We do not realise how precious we are to Jesus. Remember, when a human child suffers a minor harm, the child's parents suffer much greater than whatever pain was caused to the child. When we talk about our sonship with the Father, we compare it with the earthly physical relationship in order to proximate the concept. However, our relationship is much greater: "... that they all may be one, as You, Father, are in Me, and I in You; that they also may be one in Us". He speaks about a love and Oneness beyond the comprehension of the world. Becoming His children is not the same as physically having children on Earth. This is a different relation—one stemming from Christ's sonship with the Father. This is a concept beyond our intellectual comprehension. It is the status in which God wishes to place the Church, whereby when Christ ascends to Heaven with her, she will be glorified at the right hand of the Father.

Perhaps, when Saul saw the light and heard the voice ("It is hard for you to kick against the goads"), this was the Light of Resurrection in his life. However, the Light blinded Saul, because Resurrection is to be preceded by death. Buried with Christ in Baptism: as we are raised from among the dead, we also walk in the new life. No one is worthy of the blessing of the Resurrection, except those who taste death with Christ, where death is the elimination of love of the world and bodily desires, thus elevating our minds to heaven.

How Does One Gain Sonship?

This is an important question for those who speak of salvation. Can anyone attain salvation on their own? In Saul's case, he was told that he would be guided to the Church at Ananias. The Church was intimidated by Saul, who was notorious for his persecution and removal of people, but God appeared to Ananias and asked him to receive Saul, and Ananias opened the door for him.

Saul believed Christ was the Son of God. He was told he would have to be baptised, and Saint Paul was baptised on that same day. Immediately, scales started to fall off Saul's eyes and he began to see. This is one of the beautiful aspects of Baptism: it brings insight into the blinded soul. In this case, the eyes that were given sight were eyes of the new Resurrection, and saw our Lord. In the miracle of the Blind Man, Jesus was the first person the Blind Man saw upon opening his eyes when he gained sight. The Blind Man saw Him physically standing before him, but he also gained insight, enabling him to receive Christ in his life.

The Holy Gospel demonstrates experientially that Saint Paul was only able to receive Christ through the Church and Baptism: that is, by opening his sight, whereby he saw Jesus. When reading this story in Acts, you may notice that Saint Paul recounted this story often, wherever he went. Whenever he was asked, he said, "I shall tell you my story. I was on my way, I was resisting our Lord, and then—". Saint Paul was recounting the story of his Resurrection, the story of his new birth and how he became God's son. He narrated the story of how he lost his sight, symbolising his past life, telling how he was blind both in sight and insight. How, through the Church, he received the sacrament of Baptism and could see immediately—he had Christ's light for the rest of his life.

This is the way for God's children: "I am going to prepare a place for You with my Father". When they asked Him if that place was made of rooms joined to each other, He tried to explain to them that it was a place where they would be with His Father, where they would become His children, and if they became His children, He would come to take them.

They asked Him, "Why not now; why wait?" He told them that, after Baptism, they were anointed with the ointment of detachment from the world. They were no longer the children of the world—anointed with the ointment of the Heavenly Father, they had become God's Children. They were to remain in the world until they matured, as it was said in Hebrews: "let us consider one another to provoke unto love and to good works", abstaining from evil and becoming Heaven's Children.

When Jesus spoke about knowing the Way, He did not mean that He would come to take us when we die and a funeral is held for us, thus concluding our way. No: He will come and take us upon our comprehending the Father's paternity of us, when we become embedded in Him. "...he who loves Me will be loved by My Father, and I will love him and manifest Myself to him". He will manifest Himself to us, showing us that He is the Son of God. This is how the Way is explained, but some people are unable to comprehend it. When understood, the Way will be known, and we will become God's Children.

When Phillip heard this, the first thing that came to his mind was to say: "Show us the Way or show us the Father, and it is sufficient for us". Thomas also said, "Show us the way", to which Jesus replied, "I am the Way. My teachings are the Way. They are the guide which will show you how to reach the Father".

Where is Christ? He says, "I am with you to the end of times". That is why the Resurrection is fulfilled when we discover God's paternity. It is not enough that we say, "We are raised with Christ". We need to feel that we are God's children. Our ascension is not linked to the ascension of our souls to Heaven on the day of our death. Saint Paul speaks in the past tense ("and raised us up together and made us sit together in the heavenly places in Christ Jesus") (Ephesians 2:6). Then, he adds that our life (meaning our life and our behaviour on Earth) is written in Heaven. It reminds me of the satellites that are flown from Earth using radars, remote controls, or some other type of electronic mechanism.

Being on Earth, we are moved from above because we are the children of the Father. Someone drew an analogy: when an infant is born of the womb, the umbilical cord is cut, severing the infant's physical tie to the mother. When we were born in Baptism, however, we remained children of the Heavenly Father; the cord tying us to the Heavenly Father was not severed. We can reach Him at any moment. We cannot reach our biological parents at any moment, but we can reach our Heavenly Father. We can remain without separation from Him—not for a moment, not for a blink, not while we are awake, not while we are at work, not at Church, or in the street—anywhere, anytime, He is our Heavenly Father.

This is the constant movement of ascension described by Prophet David: "The steps of a good man are ordered by the Lord: and he delighted in his way" (Psalm 37:23). Across the ages, through the transparency of his spirit, David perceived that ascension could be an inner movement inherent within the heart. "The steps … were ordered by the Lord … and he delighted in his way".

Following the Way is being God's children. Once this feeling grows, it develops into an impetus in our life, driving us into being the Lord's Children. We received this feeling in our Baptism. However, this feeling should be within us at all times—a feeling that we are nestled in our Lord's bosom, always in His care, always following His precepts—because we are His children. We do not commit evil because we are in the image of our Heavenly Father, and people glorify our heavenly Father when they see our good deeds. In this way, the cord between us is never severed.

We are not influenced by the world. People often make the mistake of saying we are influenced by our environment. This applies to those who are not tied to Heavenly Paternity, but not to those whose Father is in Heaven and who live according to the precepts, teachings and guidance of the Father. A good son chooses to be an image of his father. This is the Way.

When Phillip said, "Show us the Way", He replied "Goodness Phillip! I have been with you all this time, and you don't know Me! I am in the Father and the Father is in Me! The Way is where I wish to place you so as to make you Children of the Father". Saint Paul confirms this point: "Therefore, brethren, having boldness to enter the Holiest by the blood of Jesus, by a new and living way which He consecrated for us, through the veil, that is, His flesh" (Hebrews 10:19). The Church is our Way; it is constant contact with the Heavenly Father.

Perhaps, now we can understand more clearly what our Lord meant when He said, "Assuredly, I say to you, unless you are converted and become as little children, you will by no means enter the Kingdom of Heaven" (Matthews 18:3). Children are innocent, pure at heart, and good: God wants us to become like them. No one can say "Mama" or "Papa" with such innocence, love and heartfelt affection as a child. That is why our Lord wants us to be like children. Christ wants to tell us that it is when we reach that state that we know the Way. When we know how to say the Word with the same love and sincerity, then we can say, "Our Father who art in Heaven ..." This is when we know how to reflect on this prayer. When the Disciples asked Christ, "Teach us how to pray", He taught them the example to follow whenever they prayed. Be Holy, because your Father is Holy.

Our Father who art in Heaven, hallowed be your Name.

Seek our Lord's Kingdom, not the earthly kingdom. Be concerned with the Heavenly issues and the spread of our Lord's Kingdom and say, "Our Father, Your Will be done". We should aspire to reach a state of praying like Christ did in Gethsemane: "Father, if it is Your will, take this cup away from Me; nevertheless, not My will, but Yours, be done" (Luke 22:42). It is a blessing when a child grows up embracing the Father's Will (and not their own) throughout their life, becoming holy, as a Child of the Kingdom. This is the Way.

Therefore, there is no other way to the Father except through Christ. Why? Because Christ is the Father's Son by virtue of His nature—by virtue of being the Word. We became members of Christ's Body. Christ took this body, and with it He consecrated a Heavenly way and entered the Higher Holies. Thus, we became God's Children.

My dearly beloved, may God bless us with the grace of the constant ascension within our hearts, so that our life on earth may be in a constant state of sonship and may our link to heaven be greater than our link to earth.

Last Sunday (Vespers)
I Will Not Leave You Orphans

For Christians, the Pentecostal Period is like completing a journey of one thousand kilometres. After travelling 999 kilometres, the traveller remains one kilometre short of their destination. It cannot be said, at this point, that the traveller has reached their destination. Christ's final kilometre is described by the Church: "He raised our first fruit to Heaven, taking our body in His incarnate form, and seated it at the right hand of the Father". He fulfilled everything.

Christ came to the world and became incarnate not in order to save us from sin, nor in order to answer our prayers each time we call for help. Suppose He forgave us sin. What then? Christ came down to take the Church and place it at the right hand of the Father. He told His Disciples to remain in their place because there was an important issue that needed to be concluded. They told Him that He had done everything: He died on the Cross, He took our body, died in it, and was resurrected with it. What more? He told them that He was on His way to send them the promise of the Father (the Holy Spirit). He added that He would reveal to them a mysterious fact applicable to Christians only, because they are not slaves but the Children of the King. He will go to send them the Spirit of the Father, the promise of the Father—He who proceeds of the Father.

When the promise of the Father descends on them, and dwells within them, this spirit of the Father will witness for them that they are the Children of God. On that day, they are not to ask Him for anything, because the Father Himself loves them, and His spirit is present with them. He told them not to assume that all was accomplished. When they asked, He told them that He would send the Holy Spirit who proceeds from the Father to dwell within each one, whereupon they become our Lord's Children, with nothing to fear.

Christ the Lord's original aim was to declare us to the paternity of His Father. The original aim of the coming of the Holy Spirit on Pentecost was for the spirit of the Father to dwell within us, rendering us worthy of calling Him "Our Father, Abba".

This sequence of events was planned so that we may eventually become the Children of our Lord. When Adam was expelled from Paradise, he consequently lost his rank of being able to hear the voice of our Lord. By his nature as God's obedient creation, he ended up with a yearning to be with God. Then, in this new stage of grace, Christ would not allow us to return to our previous status in Paradise, but allowed us instead to be His children. Our Lord's paternity is not mere talk—that He called us, or adopted us. He poured His spirit into us, which is the Spirit of the Father.

John's Gospel: Chapters 14 to 17

Christ began to talk openly and awesomely with His Disciples about the Father. As Christians, we have the Holy Spirit within us. Even so, up to now we have been unable to fathom its depth because we have not given the Holy Spirit the opportunity to work in our lives, to reveal to us the nature of the Father.

Early on, He did not speak of the Father. This perplexed the disciples, leading Thomas to ask, "Show us the Way". He said, "How do I show you the Way?" In Christianity, the Way is one: The Father loves the Son, the Holy Spirit is the Spirit of Love, the Father and the Son are One, I am in the Father and the Father is in Me. Therefore, which is the way that leads to the Father?

Our Lord Jesus phrased it simply: "Do not trouble yourself". The way leading to the Father is not cleverness, nor is it intellectual; it was the Father Himself who sent His Son (the Word of the Father), and who became incarnate in our body. He took this Body and rose with it to the right hand of the Father, then sent to us the Spirit of the Father to dwell within us. This is the Way. Is it clear now why, when Thomas asked, "Show us the way", Christ answered, "I am the Way"? He made it clear to Thomas that there was no other way for humankind to return to the embrace of the Father and comprehend His paternity except through His incarnation—attachment to our body—through rising with it to Heaven, and sending the Holy Spirit from the Father to dwell within us. This is the Way. The Way was not through human ability or effort.

For this reason, we became God's Children, and despite the paradox, the parents are not indebted to their son. He cannot claim, "You were not the ones who brought me, I brought myself". They would say, "Son, we were the ones who brought you". They said, "Show us the Way". Which way? For what purpose? For the purpose of becoming a good, righteous, God-fearing person? No: the Way means to be included in the census of our Lord's Children and be born from above. This was a procedure meticulously calculated by Christ. The first motive was love, because supposedly the relationship of the Father and His children is one of love. This is the relationship that binds them together: "For God so loved the world that He gave the only begotten Son" (John 3:16). Our Lord mentioned this specific verse when He spoke with Nicodemus about how we should be born from above, when Nicodemus asked Him how to gain entry to our Lord's Kingdom. He explained to him that it was a regular kingdom with a gate, and the good people would be dealt with, and then judged, before gaining entry.

The Kingdom of our God is the Kingdom of the Loved Son. Jesus said, "How then, Nicodemus, will you enter to be a son?" Nicodemus asked whether it meant he would have to re-enter his mother's womb.

Jesus began to explain that in Christianity, the Kingdom is understood within the concept of birth. To join the Kingdom of our Lord, you must be born of our Lord—born of the water and spirit through Baptism. However, the power and impact of this birth is through Christ only. Because "I gave my only Son", so that He unites with you, dies for you, resurrects with you, and takes you to heaven. There is no other way to know our Lord.

We defined the meaning of knowing our Lord. He gave us his Paternity; thus, we became His children. There is no path to comprehend the Lord other than Christ. Any other way would be false sonship. It is like picking someone from the street at random and saying, "Son, as from today, I shall call you my son, and henceforth you call me 'father'". Is this the way the Lord wants us to deal with people? Some may argue that "the whole creation is God's children". No: this sonship is genuine, through which we comprehend the Father's love for us.

For this reason, while reading chapters 14 to 17, you may come across the word "love" often, in a sign of God's Paternity. "By this all will know that you are My disciples, if you have love for one another" or, "You will be my disciples. Be steadfast in my love". In concluding these four chapters, Jesus says: "Father, I want that the love with which You loved me may be in them, and I in them".

We take on attributes of Christ. He speaks of the Holy Spirit: "... take of what is mine and give to you". The Father loves the Son because this is a "love of Oneness", since the Father and the Son are one. Jesus says that He wants us to be one in Him as He is one in the Father. This means we will be recipients and participants in many aspects, and this is Divine.

Sonship means that a father is not instructed: for example, telling him to "give your child the same love you received from your father". No. The moment the infant becomes your own flesh and blood, surprisingly, you feel the surge of love.

The Father loves the child even when he misbehaves. "I love him since he is my son".

All that we receive from the Father, we receive through Christ: "For you died, and your life is hidden with Christ in God" (Colossians 3:3). In other words, our needs are "hidden with Christ in God". How then, are we to receive glory? In other beliefs or ideologies (for example, the Pharaohs) those who do some good, regardless how little, will receive a reward, and those who do evil will receive punishment. There will be a trial—judgement for the whole world. However, I am talking about glory, and the glory belongs to us, by virtue of our being the children. We are in Christ and we will live in His glory, not because it is ours in the first place, but because, since we became one in Christ, we became worthy of enjoying it. All we received from our Lord, we received through the Holy Spirit consequent to our union with Christ.

Jesus said that without the dwelling of the Spirit within us, we cannot be His Children. The first verse in chapters 14, 15, 16, and 17 says, "Let not your heart be troubled". This verse was repeated often in these chapters. He said to the Disciples that, when He told them He was leaving them to join the Father, their hearts were saddened. Thus, He said, "Let not your heart be troubled". What does this mean? It is an indication that one has God's spirit within. Why, then, should I fear? I should not fear, because the Lord takes care of me. Am I the one who takes care of the Spirit within me, or is it the Spirit of the Father who takes care of me? Am I the one who defends myself, or is He the one who defends me?

This verse is of great comfort, especially during hard times or during times of persecution, times when Satan draws pictures of dark days to come. Then, with the Spirit of the Father dwelling within us, we say, "Let not your heart be troubled". We may ask, "And why not?" Because we are reassured: "... believe also in Me. In My Father's house are many mansions... I go to prepare a place for you. And if I go and prepare a place for you, I will come again and receive you to Myself that where I am, there you may be also. And where I go you know, and the way you know". He reminds us of when He told us not to fear those who kill the Body. My Paternity means that I will take you so that you become My children, forever.

Let not your heart be troubled: never fear, because no one can violate your sonship with the Father. This led Paul to say, while he was in prison: "Who shall separate us from the love of Christ?" (Romans 8:35). I'll go even further: if we commit a sin, will the Spirit of Paternity—the Spirit of the Father dwelling within us—depart from us? Never. It will never depart from us, even if someone denounces Christ, pretends he is not Christian, and leaves Christianity, but returns repentantly asking to be re-baptised. In this instance, we will tell him we cannot re-baptise him, because God's spirit never departed from him. He may ask, "Where, then, was God's spirit?". The answer: it was grieving. For this reason, the Bible says, "And do not grieve the Holy Spirit of God, by whom you were sealed for the day of redemption" (Ephesians 4:30). The Holy Spirit does not abandon anyone, not even sinners.

If the Holy Spirit departs from the sinner upon weakening, we would not be able to repent: "And when He has come,

He will convict the world of sin, and of righteousness, and of judgment" (John 16:8). He is the one who leads us to repentance through remorse. He is the one who returns us to the Bosom of our Father. He moved the Prodigal Son towards returning to his Father.

I wish to make it clear: sonship with the Father is not simple. The Father will not give up on His children. Therefore, He says, "Let not your hearts be troubled". Be sure that you are physically in His care. Even if they kill the body, Jesus went and prepared a place for us.

Jesus wishes to place us in a greater glory. What is greater than, "... that where I am, there you may be also"? What about the spirit of paternal love? Ask any father what makes him happy. He will tell you, "When my child is in my lap". Ask a child what makes him happy. He will tell you, "When I am with my father". It is true that a father is responsible for the material needs of the child, and the child is also happy to receive his father's material gifts, but the greatest joy is when both are in each other's arms and in each other's company.

This is the aim of the Holy Spirit for our lives—but it is hardly achieved, because often we are not good. We notice in John chapters 14 to 17, in His Farewell Sermon, that Christ says, "they all may be one, as You, Father, are in Me, and I in You; that they also may be one in Us, that the world may believe that You sent Me. And the glory which You gave Me I have given them, that they may be one just as We are one: I in them, and You in Me" (John 17:21-23).

The fact is that even with the presence of the Holy Spirit within us, we spend little time with Him and then stay away for long periods: we are preoccupied with worldly concerns: the high cost of living, politics, gossip, world problems, current events. We then wake up to ourselves and say, "Let us spend some time with the Lord"—and we do so for limited time.

The Holy Spirit does not rest unless the son is always nestled in his Father's Bosom. The Saints put this into practice but, even if we fail to put this into practice in our life on Earth, we shall practise it with our Lord when we lie in His eternal Bosom.

The first point to which Jesus draws our attention is: "Let not your hearts be troubled". Never, ever give in to fear, even if our human weakness draws us to fear. Remember, Jesus is there for us. For my part, I will never forget the righteous Father Mikhail Ibrahim. In one of our meetings, he asked: "Who cleans the house? Is it the occupant or does the house clean its own walls?". Naturally, I answered: "The occupant cleans the house". Then he said: "This occupant is the Spirit of the Father who lives within the house. Who makes you our Lord's child? Is it you, or is it the spirit of The Father who is within you?"

Who is the One who purifies us of sin? Who protects us? Who equips us? It is the spirit of the Father who dwells within us. You can grasp this point when speaking about the Father. Note that there is a duality whenever there is a mention of "the Holy Spirit" and "the Father". The duality is this: "Let not your hearts be troubled", and He proceeds from the Father, because He is the Spirit of the Father.

It is a fact that Christ will "send", and there is a difference between "to send" and "to proceed". "To send" means to take something and forward it, but "to proceed" is a natural process. For example, light proceeds from a lamp. The lamp remains as it is, while the light proceeds from it. Thus, the Father is God's Spirit, and the Spirit proceeds from Him.

The Son became incarnate in our body, and this means we became part of the Holy Spirit—Who proceeds of the Father. The Father is infinite, the Holy Spirit is infinite, and the Holy Spirit infinitely proceeds in its infinite dwelling within the infinite Son. This means that it was not possible that the Holy Spirit would proceed from the Father to a human offspring of Adam (to someone like you or me). Christ became incarnate in our bodies, and we became members of His Body. The proceeding of the Holy Spirit of the Father to the Son gave us the share in Jesus Christ.

Our Church is alert to this fact, and abides to "the Holy Spirit" who proceeds from the Father. Other denominations of western churches maintain that the Holy Spirit is the Spirit of the Father and the Spirit of the Son. Therefore, the Creed of Faith should include the Son (thus, "proceeds from the Father and the Son") but we say "no". It proceeds of the Father in the Son. We do not repeat, "of the Father and the Son" because it is obvious. In other words, God's Spirit is infinite. How is it possible to proceed from the Father and from the Son? Settle in what? In a finite human? It is an infinite Spirit, proceeding from an infinite Father, in order to dwell within the infinite Son.

Our share of the Holy Spirit is the portion of our union in

Christ, which we received through His incarnation. Now, let us interpret this step by step, so that I may show you how to follow these chapters.

- "Let not your hearts be troubled".

- "Do not be afraid".

- "I go to prepare a place for you".

- "In My Father's House are many mansions".

What type of place is Jesus preparing for us in Heaven? Is it a high-rise building? Is it residential apartments? No: Jesus promised us that it will be at the right hand of the Father, which will be through our partnership in His own Body, which is the Church. We may ask, "Jesus prepared a place for the Church; where, then, is my place?" Now, I know the location of my room. I am a member of Christ's body, and Christ ascended to Heaven and sat at the right hand of the Father. My room is at the right hand of the Father. Do you see the sequence?

"Let not your hearts be troubled", for "I go to prepare a place for you".

This place is not some kind of tangible concept; this place is at the right hand of the Father.

However, if I gauge this place by tangible standards, I know where it is. It is mine. I know the apartment number; the contract is signed. I am confident about the whole deal because I am His child. This is the meaning of, "I go to prepare a place for you". I know the real meaning of this promise. He is going to make us children of our Lord, because at the outset, we had no place within our Lord's paternity. That took place only when we were united with His Body and He was united with ours, and He ascended with that Body to Heaven at the right hand of the Father. He prepared a place for us at the right hand of the Father and His spirit dwelt within us (the Promise of the Father). In this way, we received our status. Now, I know, and I am sure of my place and status as the child of our Lord.

Let us pause and think for a moment: if we reflect profoundly on this concept, then there is no difference between our living in Heaven or on Earth, and our living here or in South Africa, or living here or in another house. We reach a state of being members in the Body of Christ. Our place is determined, it is known: it is at the right hand of the Father, and the Spirit of the Father dwells within us.

"I go to prepare a place for you". You may ask, "How do we know the way?" As I explained earlier, we will go through the relevant chapters, one verse at a time. Jesus Himself answered immediately: "I am the Way". What are the requisites to be 'the Way'? The condition of having a place: we need the Paternity of the Father, and the dwelling of His Spirit within us. This was possible only when Christ became incarnate in our body, and He ascended to Heaven with this Body, thus actually becoming the Way ("I am the Way").

Then, He continued: "No one comes to the Father except through Me". They may have thought, "How does that work? Is it a filtering process?" No: there is no preferential treatment. It is because no one can ascend to the right hand of the Father, except the Son. Those who unite with the Son will have a place there, and those who do not will have no place. This is not inequity on the part of Christ—as He said, "No one comes to the Father except through Me".

"If you had known Me, you would have known My Father also" (John 14:7). How could they know Him? If they wished to know Him, they needed to use their common sense. How could they do that though? What intellect is capable of conceiving God? Had they really known Him, being the Son of the Father, they would have known the Father, and they would have understood what it means to be "at the right hand of the Father".

Within this concept, "knowledge" is the knowledge of union with Christ. For this reason, when Jesus speaks of "knowledge", He refers to the Holy Spirit as being the source of knowledge in terms of preaching, guidance and reminding. The Holy Spirit explains the Father to us, takes of Christ, and gives to us.

At this point, what we mean by "knowledge" takes a U-turn. Instead of "knowledge" meaning human knowledge of God, it is now the Holy Spirit who is pouring into the human according to their capacity. It is according to the richness of our Lord, and according to what extent our hearts are receptive.

What is the gauge of "knowledge" of our Lord? A simple person, with scant worldly knowledge—even an illiterate person—can, at the same time, have great knowledge of the Father if they remain steadfast in Christ and behave accordingly. Christ's promise stands.

Of course, the whole issue is intricate. In the same chapter, Christ says, "If anyone loves Me, he will keep My word; and My Father will love him, and We will come to him and make Our home with him" (John 14:23). If this love is the indication of knowing our Lord, then our Lord's love will be poured within our hearts through the Holy Spirit, and we arrive at the doorstep of: "How do we know God?"

We know God through prayer and the outpouring of ourselves that accompanies it—through humility, through love, and through many other factors that do not occur to our minds. Some people tell us that we know God through reading the Bible; keeping our mind occupied; reflecting on nature, Heaven and Earth; through speaking of our Lord's glory; and through keeping our minds occupied.

However, I would add that when we humble ourselves—when we have love in our hearts, and we unite with Christ—our knowledge of Him will pour within our hearts. Often some people tell me, "Father, when I read the gospel now, I come to understand things I did not understand in the past; how that is?" I tell them, "This is comparative to your humility. If you are humble in the eyes of God, He will not withhold His generosity. He will pour His spirit of joy, to fill your heart with loving Him more and more". This is knowledge.

Philip told Him, "Show us the Father and that suffices". In response, He told Philip that they had seen the Father in Him, and that He was taking them with Him on his way to Heaven. He told Philip that He was with them all that time. He emptied Himself, became incarnate for them to know Him and for them to abide in Him. You will find that the sentence, "Abide in me" repeated many, many times in the aforementioned chapters, and in Chapter 15 especially.

Christ says, "I am the vine; you are the branches. He who abides in Me, and I in him, bears much fruit". In Chapter 16, He says abide in My love. When Phillip tells Him that to be shown the Father would suffice, He explains that He and the Father are One. Whoever sees Him sees the Father; He is the Way, and that's all there is to it. The verses emphasise and confirm this oneness.

"Most assuredly, I say to you, he who believes in Me, the works that I do he will do also; and greater works than these he will" (John 14:12).

Let's not stop here. As Christians, let's not stop at, "will do also". In these four chapters, you will come across many verses that Jesus follows with an immediate explanation. For example: "Do not touch me, because I am ascending to my Father" is explained as, "I did not as yet accompany you to the Father, because you are not yet a child of the Father". Jesus wanted to tell her that she was an outsider in this sense. He was implying a state of duality: "My Father and your Father until I ascend and take you up".

In this verse, He says, "the works that I do he will do also; and greater works than these he will", but how is that possible? "Because I go to My Father". The statement is followed by an explanation. Consequently, as Christians, we can do those works and even greater works, because Christ is going to the Father, whereby we are being placed at the right hand of the Father, and are able to do great works as a result. Also, when

He ascended to be at the right hand of the Father, our eyes opened to the nature of the works; they became divine and related to the Heavenly. All links to present, future, and past were severed. The upper works are much, much greater works than those on Earth, and those are the works we will be doing.

So, when He said that He was going to His Father, there was another part to the verse: "the works that I do he will do also; and greater works than these he will". How is it possible that we will be able to do greater works than those done by Christ? Because when He says that He is going to the Father, and we shall remain here, this means that our works will be greater than the Earthly works. True, we are on Earth; but where is our actual life? It is in Heaven. The Divine love and the Divine mysteries were given to us, the simple people. As a result, we began to perform great works, because our motive became Mighty and Divine. Thus, "the works that I do he will do also; and greater works than these he will"—but why?

Because I am going to my Father. The explanation is clear. "If you abide in Me, and My words abide in you, you will ask what you desire, and it shall be done for you. By this My Father is glorified, that you bear much fruit; so, you will be My disciples".

"By this My Father is glorified": does this mean that the Father is glorified by the Son? Yes. Was it not mentioned that, when people see our good deeds, they glorify our Father in Heaven? The Father is further glorified by the Son: "Those whom You gave me, I have kept..." Jesus ascended to Heaven and raised His Saints and offered them a sacrifice to His Father. Thus, the Father was glorified.

Consider this parallel. A secondary school student was preparing for his examinations. He studied hard throughout the school year, passing his final exams with an exceptionally high mark. This means he excelled: he was glorified, and so was his effort, and so were his teachers, who instructed him. They gave him the education and knowledge he needed in order to succeed. In the same way, Christ descended to the world and took our humanity. He raised us and united us with Him, elevating us, and the Father was glorified by the Son, because He raised us to Heaven. This means that Christ's mission was totally successful: "none of them is lost except the son of perdition" (John 17:12).

Now, you can carefully read the four chapters at hand, reader, verse by verse, so that you too may follow the ascension of Christ and His seating at the right hand of the Father.

"If you love Me, keep My commandments. And I will pray the Father, and He will give you another Helper, that He may abide with you forever" (John 14:15). Does "forever" mean in this world? "Forever"—with the spirit of Truth? What are the attributes of this "spirit of truth"? It is "whom the world cannot receive, because it neither sees Him nor knows Him; but you know Him, for He dwells with you and will be in you".

This is what Christ said: "the spirit of the Father, whom the world cannot receive, because it neither sees Him nor knows Him". When the world speaks of Him, it speaks out of ignorance. The perception of the world is this: What Father? What Son? This is an issue—when someone discusses this father of that son, who took for himself a female friend, resulting in a conjugal relationship, culminating with birth-giving. It's hard to explain. In contrast, we are immersed in the sublimity of the Divinity, and are rejoicing spiritually.

It was truly sweet when He said that He would not leave us orphans. Of course, children who are left without a father are orphans. Christ took the Church and seated her at the right hand of the Father, entrusting her to Him and giving her the Spirit of the Father. Thus, the Church continues to live in the Spirit of the Father. Had this not been the case, the Church would have been an orphan. Whoever does not receive the Holy Spirit in this world is an orphan because they are without a father.

"I will not leave you orphans": this means that God's paternity will include every human orphan. They will all live in the Bosom of the Father, forever and ever. Is this not the Lord's Prayer? When we pray, we say: "Our Father, who art in heaven ..."

In each verse, you will discover the Father's love for you. By the time you go through the four chapters at hand, you will understand in full the meaning of the Ascension.

Last Sunday
Jesus Has Overcome the World
(John 16:23-33)

The Lord ascended to Heaven: "He commanded them not to depart from Jerusalem, but to wait for the promise of the Father". In chapters 14, 15, 16 and 17 of Saint John's Gospel, Christ began by speaking to His disciples about the most serious issue they would ever face: "I came forth from the Father and have come into the world. Again, I leave the world and go to the Father" (John 16:28).

Why was Christ Incarnated? Why was He Crucified? And Why was He Resurrected?

He was incarnated in order to bless humanity and be among us. He was crucified out of His love for us to redeem us of our sins. He was raised in order to resurrect us with Him.

We hear a great deal about the Resurrection, but what follows it? Christ was keen on fulfilling His mission, and for this reason, He said: "Nevertheless I tell you the truth. It is to your advantage that I go away; for if I do not go away, the Helper will not come to you; but if I depart, I will send Him to you" (John 16:7). He told them that if they loved Him, they would rejoice in seeing Him go away, knowing that He had fulfilled His mission of forgiveness and redemption, that He was on His way to His Father, to place the Church on the right hand of the Father.

In the Liturgical text, the priest says: "He ascended to Heaven and sat at the right hand of His Father". We are the body of the Church: the Body of Christ. Thus, Christ ascended to Heaven and the Church sat at His right hand, the hand of might and greatness of God the Almighty. Jesus fulfilled his mission. In His farewell prayer, He told His Disciples that He did not ask the Father for their sake, because the Father Himself loved them, "and have loved them as You have loved Me".

The Paternity of God the Father

Again, He says: "I will not leave you orphans". Without a father, we were orphans. Jesus came to take the Church to comprehend the essence of paternity, to make her realise that God is her Father. This whole process was not as simple as God saying, "I chose you. You became my children".

When God, the Christ, the Word of the Father, took our body, He gave us the potential to become members of His Body and His Presence, at the right hand of the Father. In turn, this means our presence at the right hand of the Father. He being the Son of God in nature, and we being members of His body, which He took of our Lady the Virgin.

God the Father loves us immensely. He gave us His Holy Spirit: "He commanded them not to depart from Jerusalem, but to wait for the Promise of the Father" (Acts 1:4). If you carefully read these chapters, you will find that all of them rotate around "the Father". The whole idea is to bring us to comprehend God's feelings towards us. The most painful state in life is when a son lives with his father and says, "he is not my father" or "I do not feel his fatherhood".

God's Nature is Love

Christ descended from Heaven, became incarnate in our body, and died to redeem us. He ascended to Heaven in that Body in order to reveal to us God's Nature (who loves us). "You have sent Me, and have loved them as You have loved Me." (John 17:23)

Christ fulfilled His mission by saying, "But the time is coming—indeed it's here now—when you will be scattered, each one going his own way, leaving me alone. Yet I am not alone ... Each of you will go your own way and leave me all alone. Yet, I'm not" (John 16:32).

Herod, Pilate, the High Priest, the Scribes and the Pharisees all stood against the Lord. They gave Him the Cross and left Him all alone, but He says: "I am not alone, because the Father is with me". Jesus fulfilled His important mission. He placed the Church at the right hand of the Father— how did He do this? He delivered a Church washed in His noble Blood from the Cross—a sweet, pure Church. Everyone deserted Him, but He was not alone.

The Filial Spirit

"In the world you will have tribulation; but be of good cheer, I have overcome the world" (John 16:33). The material world can hurt our material needs, but when Christ ascended to Heaven with the Church (His Body), He overcame the world. The world became at the feet of the Church. He overcame Satan and arose with the Church to the right hand of the Father. The Church is glorified at the right hand of the Heavenly Father, in addition to being assured by the Father's promise—the Father who opened His heart and poured His Spirit. He did not give us any less; He gave us his Holy Spirit.

Saint Paul reassured us that we were not given a spirit of servitude, nor of fear. Rather, we were given the spirit of adoption: the Spirit of the Father, to whom we cry, saying, "Our Father, Abba". Jesus told us that He did not ask the Father for us, because He took us to Him, and now we live in the world with this deep feeling. We have a Heavenly Father who gave us His Spirit, and we move with this Spirit.

Remember: our knowledge of God is not intellectual—it is paternal. He poured His Spirit within us. It is not we who know our Lord; it is He who made His Spirit known to us. It is not the child who knows his father; it is his father who cuddles him, nurtures him, and brings him up. Then, gradually, the child begins to feel the father's love, begins to develop feelings he cannot express through his human intellect. His feelings towards his father cannot be articulated, because he feels there are no adequate words to express.

The Spirit of Knowledge

The Father poured His Spirit on us. He endowed us with knowledge beyond description. It is not the type of knowledge known to the world (i.e., through books, discussions, debates, or other worldly material sources). It is not as though God offered knowledge based on certain criteria (e.g., only to the intelligent or the educated, to those with means, to wealthy countries, or to countries with vast means to support an extensive media apparatus).

No: God is not known through similar means. He sent His Spirit to His children. The door of knowledge is wide open for all of us, because the Spirit of the Father reveals to us many issues. He takes these mysteries and passes them to His children, who become God's Children, who have divine mysteries flowing from the Father to them: "my Father will give you whatever you ask in my name".

Consider the relationship of the Son and His Father. The Father loves us; His Being was revealed to the Church, with the Church situated at the right hand of the Father and the Father endowing the Church with His Spirit. This paternity is not mere talk. It is love and pouring of the Holy Spirit.

Consider this: "My Father will give you whatever you ask in My name". I did not ask the Father for anything on your behalf, because the Father loves you.

Naturally, had the Disciples been given the chance to explain what they had asked of Him, they would have said, "We asked You for things many times, but You did not give them to us. We asked You once to send fire from Heaven and burn the

Samaritans, but You did not. On the contrary, You rebuked us. You told Peter, 'Get behind Me, Satan!' Often, we asked You to do more nice acts which people had enjoyed, like the satisfying of the crowds. You did not repeat these acts, and now You are telling us that we did not ask You for anything?"

Christ would have agreed, and said: "Yes. Because my whole aim and my whole mission is to take you to the Father. I want you to know how a son begins asking his father. At the beginning you went around yourselves, asking for yourselves or things around you. Once I moved the Church to the right hand of the Father, the Church became the one to ask the Father, because the Father loves her".

Christ's Farewell Prayer: Oneness

What did Christ ask for in His farewell prayer?

He is the Head of the Church, and the Church is at the right hand of the Father. The doors have been opened wide for her; she received the Spirit of the Father. Whatever we ask of the Father is given to us. What did Christ ask for at the end of His prayer? "Holy Father keep through Your name those whom You have given Me, that they may be one as We are" (John 17:11).

What Christ asked of the Father was the same oneness He had with Him, in order to show the world that the Father loved Him.

This might seem like an odd request: Christ is already one with the Father, but He said that "they were the ones" He was bringing with Him from the world in fulfilment of His mission, so that they would be one in Him as He was One in the Father. So, what was His relationship with the human being?

The Lord's Spirit (the Son) is One with the Father. When man was created the breath of life was blown into him. If the breath of life is taken away, man returns to dust. However, since we became members of the Son's body, we entered a state of oneness, whereby we feel the pouring of God's Spirit within us. Also, in the existence of God, we received His Spirit in the sacrament of the Baptism.

Christ tells us, "Abide in Me". This is because, when the branch is firm in the source, whatever is within the tree flows in the branches, which remain firm in the trunk.

Abiding in God

"Abide in Me": if Christians only realised the value of the gift given to them. They became members of Christ's body and are at the right hand of the Father. Whatever they ask of the Father is given to them. What would I want of the Father? I am in His embrace: I ask for oneness. Listen to what Christ says at the end of His prayer: "... and will leave Me alone". You may wonder if this is hard to do. Of course—it has a tremendous impact psychologically. He continues: "... And yet I am not alone, because the Father is with Me. These things I have spoken to you, that in Me you may have peace. In the world you will have tribulation; but be of good cheer, I have overcome the world".

How did Christ overcome the world? It was never mentioned that He held a sword or waged war, nor did some kind of fire come from Heaven but He was expected to act with authority and aggression in order to create fear among His opponents (e.g., the Scribes and the Pharisees) and for Christianity to gain status. He said, "I have overcome the world". Did the world succeed to detach Him from His Father? He was forsaken by all. He was insulted. He was left on His own. Nevertheless, He said, "And yet I am not alone, because the Father is with Me".

The Peril of Detachment from God's Embrace

What could be more perilous for a soul born within the Church than to detach from the embrace of the Father? Where did the danger lie when the Prodigal Son ventured to leave his father's home to a faraway country? In that far away country lay death, because he estranged himself from his Father's home. When he returned to his Father's embrace, however, life surged through his body. Death had no longer had authority over him. He had overcome the world and death, and he continued to do so for as long as he was in his Father's bosom.

The Church who is steadfast in Christ gets all she asks of Christ, but what is meant by "all she asks"? What about things she did not seek? "Holy Father, keep through Your name those whom You have given Me that they may be one as We are".

Christ gave us another form of prayer to the Father: "To be one in Him".

Oneness of Will

It was never mentioned that Christ had acted contrary to the will of His Father. The Two are One. You might say, "Father, this issue should never even be raised, because Christ is the Word of God".

It's true—they are one will. Some have erred and claimed, "they are two wills", but never—not even once—did we see Christ do anything contrary to the will of the Father. When He prayed, "... not My will, but Yours, be done", It was for the purpose of teaching us. "I am in the Father, and the Father in Me". This is the oneness of will and, to the same extent that you conform to the will of Christ, you are one in the Father and our Lord's Spirit abides in you.

Jesus emphasises an important point in this prayer. He says "... you did not ask for anything until now". He wants us, in order for our joy to be complete, to seek that we may receive. I know your reaction to this: "Father, the Lord gives us other things". True, and it makes us happy. Everyone enjoys worldly gifts, but that joy is not a lasting one, because it is worldly. We enjoy it for its moment, and then the novelty wears off.

"If you abide in Me, no one can take your joy from you", because this joy is the fruit of the Holy Spirit. It is the fruit of the same Holy Spirit whom the Lord poured on Pentecost. He gave it to us (the Church) being members of the Body of Christ. It is the comforting spirit whose main fruit is joy. No one can take it from us because (and bear this in mind) it became part of the Church who is at the right hand of the Father. It is not a worldly joy, as we shall see now.

Love

Consider what Christ asked for in His farewell prayer: "the love with which You loved Me may be in them, and I in them". This is very important; now we are receiving the gifts that belong to Christ, as given by the Father. We are receiving these now, through the pouring of the Spirit whom we received in the Baptism, because we are members of Christ's body.

Through the Holy Spirit, we receive what is of the Father. The Holy Spirit takes what is of Christ and gives it to us. Why? "That the love with which You loved Me may be in them, and I in them". This means that now when we pray and seek, we do not ask nor receive on a standard level. God anticipates these needs and He satisfies them in abundance. God elevates us as His children, as a Church, at the right hand of the Father. He raises us above much, much higher than the level of this world.

Attachment to Christ

Jesus taught us to pray seeking oneness. "Abide in Me so that all become one in Me as I am in you". We begin by seeking never to separate from Him, not even for a split second—not for a twinkling of an eye—so that we may live the eternal life. We begin by seeking the love of the Holy Spirit within us. Our teacher Saint Paul says, "Because the love of God has been poured in our hearts by the Holy Spirit who was given to us" (Romans 5:5). Yet when Paul said this, he himself was going through a great ordeal.

He spoke of "boasting in ordeal", meaning that he was experiencing an ordeal at the time, or a great ordeal that brought him patience. In the process, a love like none before was poured into his heart. It was not a worldly love or a human love. It was not of the same nature as a father's love for his son, or a brother's love for his sibling, nor even a husband's love for his wife. It was a Divine, great love. The Holy Spirit can pour this love into our hearts amid ordeals: "Until now you did not ask for anything".

"Ask for the things I asked for". Christ stood, asking that we be given the love His Father gave Him—not the love of the world but His own peace. What is Christ's peace? His peace is peace from being One in the Father.. That is why, in the first verse of chapter 14, in His last prayer, Jesus says, "Let not your hearts be troubled ... if I go and prepare a place for you, I will come back and take you to be with me that you also may be where I am" (John 14:3).

He reassures us: "be patient". The place He will prepare for us is not an average one. He will take the whole Church and place it at the right hand of the Father. Now, the Church has a place. Often, this topic makes us think about our own place when we die. I can tell you now: it is secure, and it is in Heaven. The Church has its place at the right hand of the Father. Thus, we have a place and we have a Father. This is our place; there is no other.

Of course, the Disciples could not comprehend this. They kept asking Him, "tell us about the Father". Perhaps, among themselves, they wondered about the nature of this place what would be prepared for them. It's human nature to think in earthly terms. Will this place be comfortable in terms of climate? Will there be trees? Will it be peaceful? Will I encounter financial problems? Will people feel tired? Will there be disease? Will there be total peace?

What the Father told them was entirely different: this place is at the right hand of the Father. It is an eternal place, in perpetual oneness.

Heavenly Peace

When we seek, we are to seek heavenly peace, not earthly peace. He can protect and manage our affairs, and even the hairs on our head are numbered by Him. We can call upon Him in the day of trouble: "Call upon Me in the day of trouble; I will deliver you, and you shall glorify Me" (Psalm 50:15). However, this is not the purpose for which He came. He came to place the Church at the right hand of the Father.

When Christ stood for prayer, He said, "I do not pray that You should take them out of the world, but that You should keep them from the evil one" (John 17:15).

Had the whole point merely been to prepare a physical place for us when we die (or, according to some people, to prepare a place for when He comes to take our souls to Heaven), He would not have said, "I do not pray that You should take them out of the world, but that You should keep them from the evil one". The place is established. Now, our place is in the bosom of the Father, and all that Christ wishes to say on this topic is, "... that You should keep them inseparable from You ... to be one with You; to be filled of love for You".

Spiritual Apathy

What is the imminent danger facing us at present? It is the evil one: "I do not pray that You should take them out of the world, but that You should keep them from the evil one". We are threatened with separation from Him. We are threatened by the diminishing love of our Father, and this the worst thing that can happen.

This is a complaint from which we suffer constantly; at times we do not know how to pray or how to approach our Lord. Our talk is reduced to human emotions. We talk about apathy— particularly spiritual apathy, but what is meant by "spiritual apathy" towards the Father? His Spirit is within us. So, what is the source of this spiritual apathy? Even the Bible tells us in Revelation: "Nevertheless I have this against you, that you have left your first love. Remember therefore from where you have fallen; repent and do the first" (Revelation 2:4).

Seek love: "I do not pray that You should take them out of the world, but that You should keep them from the evil one". Christ prayed for oneness, He prayed for love to be poured into us through the Holy Spirit, and for this Holy Spirit to give us the joy of living in the Father throughout our life, forever and ever.

Our hearts are filled with the joy of being in the bosom of the Heavenly Father: "I do not pray that You should take them out of the world". This means that He takes life when He sees fit. Our remaining time on Earth is according to His Will, according to the purpose we are meant to fulfil. Saint Paul says that, had it been left to him, he had "a desire to depart and be with Christ, which is far better". Yet God has a purpose for each of us on Earth: how long we live on this Earth, the type of mission we are to fulfil, and so on. This is not our focus while we are here on Earth. Our focus is on our home, and our home is where we are seated now. This is a figure of speech—I do not mean that it is literally where we are seated now (whether at home, in the Church, or somewhere else altogether). No: our place is in the bosom of the Father, and our place is already established.

Being taken from this world is not an issue that preoccupies me—I don't think about whether I will live for a long time or a short time. The issue that preoccupies me "is to be kept from the evil one"—in other words, "to be kept in Oneness with the Lord".

O Holy Spirit, come and pour more love in our hearts so that each day we may be able to comprehend the Father's love, but make us realise that the Father's love is beyond our comprehension.

It is my wish that each of us may enjoy this love with joy and peace amid this world of turmoil and tribulation. May we always remember Christ's prayer: "Let not your hearts be troubled", and His promise when He said that He was on His way to the Father. Remember that He took the Church with Him. He knew that the Disciples were saddened, but He reassured them when He prayed: "I do not pray that You should take them out of the world, but that You should keep them from the evil one. They are not of the world, just as I am not of the world. Sanctify them by Your truth. Your word is truth. As You sent Me into the world, I also have sent them into the world. And for their sakes, I sanctify Myself, that they also may be sanctified by the truth".

Sanctification

"And for their sakes I sanctify Myself..." (John 17:19).

Why should Christ sanctify Himself? Is He not Holy? Of course, Christ is Holy. He is the true essence of Holiness.

This concept is not the same as the worldly concept of holiness. Sanctification is not refraining from committing sin. We consider that sanctification is steadfastness in the Holy One. If we are not steadfast in God, we are not sanctified. God is Holiness. Only He is Holiness: "for their sakes I sanctify Myself". He is the Creator.

When Christ spoke, He spoke as the Creator of the whole world; at the same time, He was sanctifying Himself for our sake: "for their sakes I sanctify Myself". They will be One in the Father and the Son. For this reason, Christ sanctified Himself. It is a serious prayer, to consecrate one's life in sanctification in God. Once life is sanctified, the sanctification radiates to others. "For their sakes I sanctify Myself ... so that they also may be sanctified". From that point onwards, Christ's prayers became repetitive and asking for more. His requests began to examine deep concepts that cannot be interpreted separately from the status given to the Church—that is, her Oneness with the Father and her placement at the right hand of the Father. For this reason, the four chapters at hand must be perused meticulously.

The chapters must be read within the understanding that Christ manifested His aim. He placed the Church in the status of the sonship that was inherent in the right hand of the Father. Christianity cannot be understood except through this concept. We became God's Children, and our place is established: at the right hand of the Father.

We are given the Spirit of the Father Himself to dwell within us. Therefore, all the gifts the Church receives are of a Divine nature. We receive sonship, we receive the Spirit of God, we receive Christ's Body and Blood, steadfastness in Him, Divine Love that pours into us. Consequently, we receive full consecration. We receive consecration of our life to God; it becomes fully sanctified. Thus, our requests become divine requests, unlike the ones we once made—because now, the Church has ascended with Christ.

Printed in the USA
CPSIA information can be obtained
at www.ICGtesting.com
CBHW032327080524
8295CB00007B/139

9 780648 281498